ABRAHAM LINCOLN

GREAT LIVES

Other volumes in preparation

ABRAHAM LINCOLN
by D. W. BROGAN

Great Lives

DUCKWORTH
3 HENRIETTA STREET
LONDON   W.C.2

First Published . *1935*

Made *and* printed *in* Great Britain
By The Camelot Press Ltd
London *and* Southampton

CONTENTS

5

CHRONOLOGY

1809.	Feb. 12th.	Lincoln born in Kentucky.
1816.		The Lincolns move to Indiana.
1818.		Mrs. Lincoln dies.
1819.		Thomas Lincoln marries again.
1830.		The Lincolns move to Illinois.
1834.		Lincoln elected to Illinois Legislature.
1837.		Lincoln admitted to Bar and settles in Springfield, Illinois.
1842.		Lincoln marries.
1846.		Lincoln elected to Congress.
1848.		Lincoln speaks in New England.
1854.		The Kansas–Nebraska Act.
1856.		Lincoln joins the Republican Party.
1858.		Candidate for Senate.
1860.		Elected President.
1861.	Mar. 4th	Inaugurated as President.
	April 14th.	Fort Sumter fired on.

1861.	July 21st.	Battle of Bull Run.
1862.	April 6th–7th.	Battle of Shiloh.
	Mar.–July.	Battles round Richmond.
	Aug. 29th–30th.	Second Battle of Bull Run.
	Sept. 17th.	Battle of Antietam.
	Sept. 22nd.	Emancipation Proclamation.
	Dec. 13th.	Battle of Fredericksburg.
1863.	May 2nd–3rd.	Battle of Chancellorsville.
	July 1st–3rd.	Battle of Gettysburg.
	July 4th.	Surrender of Vicksburg.
	Nov. 19th.	Gettysburg oration.
	Nov. 25th.	Battle of Chattanooga.
1864.	May–June.	The Wilderness.
	Aug.	The Chicago convention.
	Sept. 2nd.	Fall of Atlanta.
	Sept.–Oct.	Sheridan in the Valley. Battle of Winchester.
	Nov.	Re-election.
	Feb. 3rd.	Hampton Roads Conference.
1865.	Feb. 18th.	Fall of Charleston.
	Mar. 4th.	Second Inaugural.
	April 3rd.	Fall of Richmond.
	April 9th.	Surrender of Lee.
	April 14th.	Murder of Lincoln.

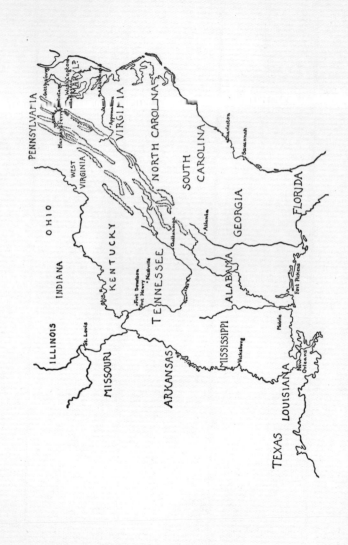

CHAPTER I

THE FRONTIER : 1809–1834

ON February 12th, 1809, a son, to be named
Charles, was born to Dr. Darwin of Shrewsbury ;
on the same day a son, to be named Abraham,
was born to Thomas Lincoln at Sinking Springs,
Kentucky. The contrast between the compara-
tive wealth, the culture, the comfort of Darwin's
environment in his childhood and the wretched
poverty, the ignorance, and the semi-savagery of
the early years of the future President is significant
as well as dramatic. Lincoln was a child of the
frontier. His paternal grandfather had left a good
farm in Virginia to settle in the new lands across
the mountains, in Kentucky's " dark and bloody
ground." The elder Abraham Lincoln was,
apparently, a good farmer and a man of moder-
ately prosperous condition both in Virginia and
Kentucky. But this did not save him from death
at the hands of an Indian who, in turn, was killed
by his son, Mordecai, who thus not only avenged
his father, but saved the life of his younger brother,
Thomas. Thomas Lincoln was a poor white, less
by birth than by natural aptitude for the shiftless,
drifting life of the type of pioneer who moved,
not because he was especially fit to combat nature,
or man, on the edge of civilisation, but because he
was unfit for life in even the half-settled society

which kept on growing up around him. As far
as Thomas Lincoln had a trade, he was a car-
penter, but, save for one brief spell, he preferred
the life of a farmer to that of a craftsman, and he
preferred the life of a hunter to that of a farmer.
In build he was sturdy, and his hair and skin were
dark. He was inoffensive and shiftless. Lincoln's
mother, Nancy Hanks, was an illegitimate child.
On her mother's side she belonged to a family for
which Thomas Lincoln was a good enough match.
Her father's name is quite unknown. Lincoln
believed that his maternal grandfather was a
Virginian planter, but the maternal ancestry of
the President is a mystery – to the annoyance of
a genealogically minded people, for it was from
his mother, probably, that he inherited his
abilities.

The world into which Lincoln was born, and
which stamped him to his death, for good and
ill, was the frontier. There institutions were new ;
men stood or fell by their personal merits. A
generation was enough to establish a family as
aristocratic. Lincoln's future opponent, Jefferson
Davis, was sent to West Point, was a gentleman,
a regular army officer, an educated man, because
his father had risen in the Kentucky in which
Lincoln's father sank. The threads of tradition
binding America to Europe were gossamer on the
frontier. Neither Lincoln's father nor mother
could read ; the world they saw was the only
world they knew. It abounded in vigour ; there
were great prizes for the energetic and the
talented, notably in politics and the law. There
were few or no barriers to white men. Six years
after Lincoln's birth, a frontiersman, with no

formal education, who had been a politician, a judge, a planter, at the head of an army as amateur as its general, had defeated, very thoroughly, a British army of Peninsular veterans led by the brother-in-law of the Duke of Wellington. The triumph of the frontiersman, incarnate in the person of Andrew Jackson, was a lodestone for the ambitious, a source of pride even for the shiftless.

But the frontier had another side. It was stripped of more than aristocratic prejudices and outworn forms. Despite gallant efforts to prove the contrary, the frontier life was in many ways nasty, brutish, and, because of Indians, malaria, and duels, often short. Amusements were crude ; superstitions were rife ; the dominant religion was emotional Calvinism, fighting with uneven success against the twin evils of fiddling and fornication. Food was plentiful. Even the shiftless Thomas Lincoln, if his farming failed him, could and did keep his family alive on game. But there was little or no money to buy even elementary luxuries. When Lincoln first went to school, his sole garment was his shirt. That was all right in summer, but in winter, until the pioneer had begun to reap the fruits of his early labours, the misery of cabin life was great. Thomas Lincoln was not the kind of pioneer who ever reaped the fruits of his labours, and, if it had depended on his father, Lincoln would have grown up in a rural slum, to become, if he failed under the ordeal, another Thomas Lincoln ; if he escaped his father, another Huckleberry Finn.

Thomas Lincoln was always on the move. He had ancestral justification for this, since only one of his paternal ancestors in America had died in the state he was born in, and not one in the same house or town. But whereas the earlier Lincolns, like the more enterprising frontiersmen, had moved on to better their condition, Thomas Lincoln moved from bad to worse. In the first ten years after his marriage he moved four times, and his last move took him out of Kentucky into Indiana. There was a dispute about land-titles, and Thomas Lincoln, whether he was in the right or the wrong, was incapable of effective resistance. He built a raft, on which he floated down the Ohio, making for Indiana, a new state covered with forest and sparsely inhabited. He began by wrecking his raft and spilling its cargo – whisky and tools. He salvaged the whisky and picked land in the forest, to which he returned, in the winter of 1816, with his family and two horses, which carried their household goods as well as the emigrants. Thomas Lincoln built a " half-faced camp " – that is, a hut with only three sides, the fourth being left open to serve as window, door, and hearth. There was plenty of game, and Thomas Lincoln loved hunting, but, with characteristic incompetence, he had chosen a spot where there was no well nearer than a mile. Next year they grew a little corn (maize), and other members of the clan began to settle near them. In the autumn of 1818 came the " milk sick," which killed, among others, Nancy Lincoln.

Sarah Lincoln, age thirteen, did the woman's work. Thomas Lincoln did a little carpentry for the neighbours – but most of the time he hunted. That winter, Lincoln went to his first school, where he can have learned very little, but he now got a chance of far more educational value than Schoolmaster Crawford could offer. Thomas Lincoln went back to Kentucky and proposed marriage to his first love, now a widow. Mrs. Sarah Johnston accepted him – why, it is hard to say – and they were married on December 2nd, 1819. The new Mrs. Lincoln was rich in furniture and she was capable. She forced Thomas Lincoln to make the cabin habitable, to put a wooden floor on the earth and greased paper for a window. She washed the children, and one of them never forgot the revolution she wrought. Most important of all, though she could not read, she brought some books : *Robinson Crusoe*, *Sinbad the Sailor*, *Pilgrim's Progress*, and *Æsop's Fables*. Thomas Lincoln, who had become a Baptist just before leaving Kentucky, bought a Bible ; a little later a kinsman brought Bailey's *Etymological Dictionary* to the settlement, and Abraham Lincoln was now fit to use them all. He went for a few months to the school of Azel Dorsey, and there he learned to read and write and spell, the last an accomplishment much admired on the frontier. In 1826 he again went to school for a short time, but his total schooling lasted less than twelve months. Many legends have grown up about his precocious interest in learning, but in truth reading fascinated him. He was lazy, where his father was merely shiftless ; he would rather talk or recite or read than work ; but his amiability and charm secured tolerance for his eccentricities from everyone except his father, who apparently disliked him and whom his son disliked. Abraham's refusal to be converted to any of the religions available on the frontier marked him off from his pious father, and whatever slight chance there might have been of making a farmer of him was lost after a trip on a flat boat down the Mississippi to New Orleans had shown him the great world. It was 1828, the year that Andrew Jackson was elected President, and Abraham, like his family and like all his class, was a Jackson man. Politics were one of the great frontier diversions, and in this presidential campaign politics were more exhilarating than ever. The election of General Jackson showed what dazzling opportunities America was offering to the poorest of her sons. Next year, Thomas Lincoln prepared to move again, to leave Indiana for Illinois, a state even rawer and newer.

While the Lincoln family were thus slowly moving west, a storm cloud was growing in the South. When the Union was formed, all the states but one recognised negro slavery, but, except in South Carolina and Georgia, it was declining, and the egalitarian philosophy of the eighteenth century condemned it to the defensive. Even so unsentimental a man as Washington regarded slavery as a great wrong, and as an unprofitable form of property, and he emancipated his slaves by will ; and Jefferson had declared, " I tremble for my country when I reflect that God is just ; that His justice cannot sleep for ever." But the hopes that slavery would die a natural death were shattered when cotton culture, thanks to inventions in America and England, became immensely profitable. Slavery decayed where it was unprofitable and flourished where it paid : and in 1820 Jefferson's old fears were awakened by the " alarm bell " in the night. The new state of Missouri wanted admission with slavery, but the northern majority in the lower House of Congress opposed. Sectional interests were an old story in America. A few years before, New England had almost left the Union because of its opposition to the war with England, and moral sentiment had only a part in the conflict. But the passions revealed on both sides in the Missouri question were alarmingly bitter, and the " Missouri Compromise " – that there should be no slavery north of 36° 30′ except in Missouri – was taken as a sacred pledge by both sections that the ghost of slavery would be laid. But all Lincoln's life it continued to walk.

In March 1830 the Lincoln family entered Illinois, after a dreary march through icy rivers and desolate forest ; a horse, a wagon, four oxen, a little money, and a little store of tools and household goods made all their capital.

On a bluff on the Sangamon River fifteen acres were broken in and fenced by rails, which Abraham helped to split, and a log cabin was built. In it all had to pass the next winter, which was extraordinary in its severity ; all the bigger wild animals except the wolves died of cold. But the pioneers survived this natural siege and, when the spring came, John Hanks and Abraham got a chance to take a flat-boat down to New Orleans ; they had to build their own boat, which took six weeks, but New Orleans was reached at last, and, according to John Hanks, Lincoln was embittered by the horrors of slavery as he saw them in the great city. " The iron entered his soul," said Hanks thirty years later. There is no evidence that anyone else saw the wound at that time.

BL

But slavery *was* a wound, for the whole nation, and a wound daily more envenomed. On January 1st, 1831, William Lloyd Garrison published the first number of *The Liberator*, preaching the doctrine that holding slaves, or holding fellowship with slave-holders, was a sin ; and each year he made converts in the North – few indeed, but enough to rouse terror and anger in the South. The growth of radical opinions in both sections – the unlimited condemnation of slavery and slave-holders in one, the unlimited defence of slavery, not as a necessary evil, but as a positive good, in the other – was steady year after year ; but it had not yet reached southern Illinois, where the most important result of Lincoln's trip to New Orleans was the offer of a job. Denton Offut, who had hired him for that trip, was much impressed by Lincoln and asked him to manage the store he planned to open in New Salem. Lincoln was scrupulously honest and sober, useful qualities in a store clerk, but he had other qualities which life at New Salem enabled him to display. Near at hand was the home of the " Clary Grove Boys," a rowdy but harmless gang of farmers' sons whose leader was celebrated for his abilities as a wrestler. Offut backed his clerk to beat Jack Armstrong, the challenge was accepted, and the contest ended in a draw. This may have been a blow to Offut, but it was excellent for Lincoln, for the gang could admire him without resentment, and there was much to admire. There was his immense strength ; he had not enough of the combative spirit to be a first-class fighting man, but he could perform all kinds of feats of strength, which were currency

with which to buy friends and supporters on the
frontier. He was, in addition, very good company : although he did not drink, he had no
dislike of those who did ; he was full of stories
and jests of a type widely appreciated, the delight
of children as well as men ; and he could read !
Such a man was bound to go into politics, and
the support of the Clary Grove Boys was Lincoln's
springboard, as similar support has been of many
American politicians since ; they were his
" machine." Offut had added a mill to his store,
but neither prospered, and Lincoln was soon out
of a job. Naturally, then, he agreed to the
suggestion that he run for the legislature. Party
lines were just beginning to be drawn in the West
between the "Jackson men" and the "Clay
men," the Democrats and the Whigs to be.
Lincoln's family, like most of their class, were
staunch Jackson men, and they remained staunch
Democrats all their lives. Lincoln already had
decided that he was a Clay man, a disciple of
" Harry of the West," of a high tariff and "internal
improvements " – that is to say, of federal aid for
local public works. It was to be a momentous
choice, but for the moment it did not matter, for
Lincoln's views of national politics were nobody's
business. His brains, his physique, his amiability,
his honesty, and his laziness, all combined to
force him into some career less arduous than
pioneer farming and Lincoln soon got a chance to
acquire another asset valuable to an American
politician, for the " Black Hawk " war, if not
notable in the history of Indian revolts, gave
Lincoln the temporary rank of captain in the
militia, much later the right to some public land,

and, for the moment, some welcome pay. Having no job, Lincoln was glad to re-enlist when his three months' service was over, and was duly mustered in by Lieutenant Robe*i*t Anderson of the United States Army. Thirty years later, Major Anderson's action at Fort Sumter was to be the immediate cause of the American Civil War.

Captain Lincoln had been noted by an eastern visitor to the war, the then great poet and powerful editor, William Cullen Bryant, but he was beaten in his legislative campaign, although he polled an astonishingly high vote for a newcomer. In partnership with William Berry, Lincoln then opened a store, whose chief merchandise was liquor, as was to be remembered by enemies when hostility to alcohol suddenly became a great political force in the 'fifties. The business, despite the demand for liquor, did not pay ; it was sold to two brothers, who ran off leaving the liabilities to Lincoln and Berry. Berry died, and Lincoln found himself owing $1,100. It took him twenty years to pay off the debt.

Lincoln's next job, after he had been out of work for some months, was that of village post-master. As postmaster Lincoln was a success, even if he kept important papers in his hat ! This habit, not at all out of place in New Salem, he never abandoned, even in Washington, to the horror of some observers and the amusement of more. To the light duties of a postmaster, Lincoln added those of surveyor, learning the rudiments of the art with difficulty, for he was not a natural mathematician, but earning money thereby, or, in some cases, buckskins to be made into trousers. Washington, too, had begun his career as a surveyor, but the obvious way out of the rut was by the law, which was to be acquired by reading. In New Salem there were many books to be mastered – first grammar, then law, always poetry, and the dangerous infidel writings of Tom Paine and Volney. Whether Lincoln had ever had any religious belief to lose is uncertain, but he was probably a Deist of the eighteenth-century type. Most of the Fathers of the Republic had been of that school, but there had been a great revival of religion since. It is a tribute to Lincoln that he was still admired and trusted by his fellows although they knew he was immune from the religious passions which were often the only diversion of the frontier. The religion of the communal hysteria that swept the frontier left him cold, but he carried away from it a grim view of life, a dependence on destiny and fate that was a kind of untheological Calvinism ; he also preserved a mastery of biblical rhythm and allusion. That he preserved any more of the religion of his class and age is improbable, unless we accept the highly unreliable testimony of Pastor Chiniquy.

Infidel or not, Lincoln ran and was elected to the legislature as the candidate of both parties. He studied law from books, and practised oratory in the abundant leisure his postal duties left him ; he was as popular as ever with the men and children and made his first doubtful ventures with women. According to insufficiently authenticated stories, Lincoln fell in love with a beautiful blue-eyed, golden-haired young woman, Ann Rutledge, who died, leaving her lover broken-hearted. The story is possible, but Lincoln may

not have loved Ann Rutledge ; if he did, she may
have preferred her first love, John McNamar ;
and, in any event, Lincoln's grief, if deep, was
short-lived.   More serious was the affair with
Mary Owens. Mary Owens first visited her
sister in New Salem in 1833, and she made a great
impression on more young men than Lincoln ;
but when she returned, Lincoln had been elected
to the legislature, this time as a regular party candidate : he had risen in the world, and was not
so easily dazzled.   What happened is a mystery.
Lincoln did propose, and was rejected – from his
own account, to his great relief, for he had proposed only from a sense of duty, since Mary was
now too fat and too old ; she had been, he
thought, thrown at his head by her family, so that
the collapse of the love-affair was a happy delivery.
The episode is significant when we remember the
circumstances of Lincoln's marriage.

CHAPTER II

POLITICS : 1834–1846

Vandalia and the Legislature – Springfield and the Bar – Mary
Todd – marriage – partnership with Herndon.

VANDALIA, the capital of Illinois, had only a
hundred houses, but New Salem had only fifteen ;
so Lincoln, when he went to the legislature, was
moving into what was, for him, an urban world,
a world far more suited to his temperament than
that of his childhood.   In the little capital
Lincoln's education was to make rapid progress.
There he encountered men of education and
ability : men like John J. Hardin, who was to be
his rival for the Whig leadership ; men like
Stephen Arnold Douglas, a New Englander, four
years younger than Lincoln, who was already,
despite his bare five feet of height, a formidable
debater, known to his admiring Democratic
followers as the " Little Giant." Not one of the
legislators in Lincoln's second term was a native
of Illinois, and there were few fixed ties or
fixed institutions. Party lines were just beginning
to be drawn rigidly, and there were votes on
national issues which gave legislators a chance to
show their mettle, but the real business of the
legislators was local and the real business of
Lincoln and his colleagues from Sangamon
County was to get Springfield made the capital of
Illinois. To gain that end they were willing to
support all kinds of mad schemes for pledging the
state credit for railways and canals, and, when a
resolution was passed deploring the subversive

activities of the fanatics who were agitating for
the abolition of slavery, Lincoln kept back his
protest, denouncing "abolitionism" but also
declaring slavery to be wrong, until its publication
could do no harm to the Springfield project.
After all, he was a politician, and a successful
politician, already leader of the Whigs in the
Lower House ; he had a duty to his party and to
his conscience, but it would have been quixotic
to damage the interests of his constituents for
the mere satisfaction of registering a protest that
could have no practical results.   Attacking
slavery, or defending the Bank of the United
States, was gallery play ; the transfer of the
capital was the real work ; and on February 28th,
1837, Springfield was chosen.   It was a great
triumph for Sangamon County and a cause of
great soreness to other cities and to many voters,
who saw in it simply a glorified job.   The day
after his legislative triumph Lincoln was admitted
to the Bar of Illinois, and a month later settled
in Springfield, where he was to live for more than
twenty years and where his body lies to-day.

In his new home Lincoln was a hero to most of
the fifteen hundred inhabitants, but he was poor
and despondent, and his oddly melancholy mien
struck observers – as well it might, for, at twenty-
eight, he seemed to have done brilliantly as
a politician, and now that he had joined J. T.
Stuart as a partner there seemed to be no reason
why he should not do equally well as a lawyer.
He had left the frontier behind and had stepped
on the stage of what was, for him, the world.

In the legislature, interest was divided between
manoeuvring to aid the national parties by

motions which were often irrelevant to the
business of the state of Illinois, and to the develop-
ment of that system of lavish public works support
of which was the price paid by Lincoln and his
associates for their victory in making Springfield
the capital. In the political manœuvres, Lincoln's debating skill got plenty of practice, and he
was able to earn the gratitude of his party by his
vigorous attacks on the banking policy of President
Van Buren. Unfortunately, the economic crisis
which added force to the Whig assault on the
Democrats in national affairs had a boomerang
effect on state politics. The panic of 1837 was
very damaging to Van Buren, but it ruined
whatever slight chances the Illinois public finances
might have had of supporting the burdens laid
upon them by the lavish expenditure on public
works. Lincoln continued to defend his pet
schemes, in face of an increasing storm of criticism,
but at last the sad truth that the great gamble had
not come off had to be faced, if not by the politicians, at any rate by the investors who had lent
money to the state and now discovered that there
was no interest forthcoming. But these local
clouds were gilded for Lincoln by the increasingly
hopeful prospects of the Whigs in the approaching
presidential election. The Democrats had now to
pay for bad times and for the tactlessness of a
newspaper which sneered at the Whig candidate,
General William Henry Harrison, for his alleged
humble origin. A mildly creditable military
career, political opinions so uncertain as to be
innocuous, and the legend that he lived in a log
cabin and drank hard cider, elected Harrison.
In the campaign, Lincoln was indefatigable, not

merely as a speaker, but as an organiser. Unfortunately, Illinois was one of the few states which
went for Van Buren, thanks to the energies and
abilities of Stephen Douglas. Yet Lincoln had
acquired merit ; a speech he had made in a joint
debate with a Democratic team which included
Douglas had been immensely admired by the
Whigs and even by their opponents. Lincoln had
also shown great parliamentary adroitness, although, on one celebrated occasion, he had been
trapped into voting when the Whig plan had been
to avoid making a quorum – and had tried in vain
to escape from a hall through a window. Had Lincoln had no more to worry about than the laughter
this misadventure caused, all would have been well.

During Lincoln's first four years in Springfield
he was happier than he was ever to be again. His
rapid political rise and his acquisition of numerous
friends, who predicted for him a brilliant future,
gave him a more optimistic view of life than his
earlier experience had seemed to justify. He
began to earn money at the Bar, where he early
established a reputation as a good jury lawyer.
But the happy course of his life was interrupted
by a failure in a department of social conduct
in which Lincoln in Springfield, as in New
Salem, was not fit to shine. Except for a few
married women, wives of his friends, Lincoln was
ill at ease in female company. He was thus
unarmed by social experience when fate threw
Mary Todd across his path. A leading Whig
politician, Ninian Edwards, son of one of the
founders of Illinois, had married Elizabeth Todd,
daughter of an eminent Kentucky family, and it
was on a visit to her sister that Mary Todd first

came to Springfield in 1837. Lincoln's partner
was himself a cousin of the Todds, and Joshua
Speed, another friend of Lincoln's, brought him
to call on Mary Todd, while he himself courted
Matilda Edwards. The Mary Todd who returned
to Springfield in 1839 was a different and more
dazzling figure than she had been two years
before. She was nine years younger than Lincoln, pretty, if not beautiful, and highly accomplished by Western standards, being able to speak
and write French. She had some talent, at any
rate a sharp tongue, and this minor Jane Welsh
caught Lincoln's attention, thereby doing him
far more harm than Jane Welsh did Carlyle.
Lincoln was not the only young man to be fascinated by Miss Todd's wit. Stephen Douglas was
a frequent visitor, and it was long believed that he
had proposed to her, but Douglas had more sense.
In Lincoln, despite his lack of small talk, his
frontier crudeness, and his deplorable family,
whose existence reminded Mary Todd that she
was contemplating marrying a Kentucky poor
white, she saw a man with a brilliant future, for
all Springfield concurred in that view, and Mary
Todd was inordinately ambitious, and reasonably
anxious to escape from a stepmother. Lincoln
proposed and was accepted, but very soon re-
pented of his rashness. He attempted to break off
the engagement, a course recommended to both
parties by their best friends, but Mary refused to
let him go. Her tears broke down his resolution,
and a day was fixed for the wedding. On January 1st, 1841, Mary Todd waited for the bride-
groom, so did her family – but he did not turn
up. This belated, if selfish, display of wisdom

delivered Lincoln, for the moment, from his fatal
entanglement, but it left him in a state of melancholy from which he never again wholly escaped.
While this repetition of the Mary Owens fiasco
was being prepared, Lincoln was neglecting his
political duties, and in the great controversy over
the Supreme Court of Illinois, a controversy in
which Douglas, on the Democratic side, shone
more brilliantly than ever, Lincoln, the astute
parliamentarian and admirable debater, was
practically a non-combatant. His friends, ob-
serving his gloom, feared suicide. " I am now the
most miserable man living. If what I feel were
equally distributed to the whole human family,
there would not be one cheerful face on the
earth." So Lincoln wrote to his partner, Stuart,
who may not have been sufficiently sympathetic
to the jilter of his cousin, for the partnership was
dissolved and Lincoln joined Stephen Logan.

Lincoln, indeed, showed either some partial
healing of his scars or a desperate desire to forget
them by proposing to Sarah Rickard, a girl of
sixteen whom he had known since her childhood.
Speed had become engaged to Miss Fanny Hen-
ning, whom Lincoln admired very deeply and,
when his friend was attacked by the same terrors
that had held Lincoln back from marriage, he
advised Speed to take the plunge. Speed's happiness seemed a testimonial to matrimony, and
gave the well-meaning Mrs. Francis, wife of
Lincoln's friend, the editor of the Springfield
Whig paper, a chance to exercise her gifts as a
matchmaker. She brought Lincoln and Mary
Todd together again. One result of this intimacy
was to involve Lincoln in the most humiliating

episode of his political life. He attacked James Shields, next to Douglas the most promising young Democrat in the state, for his prudent action as a state official in refusing to let taxes be paid in the notes of the bankrupt state bank. While in the legislature, Lincoln had been a zealous defender of the bank, and that may have accounted for the bitterness with which he now attacked Shields. But he also disliked Shields for unknown reasons, although most people of both parties found the young Irishman very likeable indeed, and his personal popularity was his chief political asset. Lincoln began the attack on Shields under the name of " Rebecca," and if the political skits published under this signature were, by modern standards, personal and unjustifiably savage, they might not have led to serious trouble if Lincoln had not allowed Mary Todd and her close friend, Julia Jayne, to exercise their wit under " Rebecca's " name. The young women went too far, and Shields was stung to reply, demanding withdrawal of the charges against his honesty. Zealous friends of Lincoln arranged a duel, which was abandoned, when the two principals met, by withdrawal of the charges by Lincoln, which, at the best, was undignified. The one bright spot was that he learned his lesson and abandoned anonymous scurrility for ever. The plunge was at last taken, and hurriedly, on November 4th, 1842, he married Mary Todd. The son of a friend, noting Lincoln's formal clothes, asked him where he was going. " To hell, I reckon."

Lincoln had drawn up for Mary Todd, before their marriage, a detailed analysis of his political support, showing that he had steadily grown more popular. That tide of popularity now turned. He had not been renominated for the legislature in 1841 ; his heart was set on election to Congress, but he had the humiliation of being passed over in 1843 in his own county in favour of E. D. Baker – of being, indeed, made a delegate to vote for Baker at the party convention, an obligation which he took unduly lightly. The nomination went to Hardin, but in 1844, at the next election, Lincoln was passed over in favour of Baker. Nor was the general political situation more gratifying, for the Whigs, in 1844, lost the Presidential election. The most brilliant politician in America, Henry Clay, was beaten by the " dark horse," Polk, and politicians again learned that pre-eminence in a party was a bar to the Presidency.

On August 1st, 1843, Robert Todd Lincoln was born, but Lincoln had little cause, apart from this, to rejoice in his marriage. Mrs. Lincoln had displayed her morbidly bad temper very soon, and, although Lincoln's marriage connected him with a powerful section of the Whig party, it weakened him with the common people – or so he thought. His partnership with Logan had not been altogether a success, for Lincoln was primarily a politician and Logan a lawyer ; but when in 1844 the partnership was dissolved, Lincoln had luck – almost the only time fortune favoured him in these years – for he secured as a partner William Herndon. Herndon was only twenty-five, but he had been a passionate admirer of Lincoln since his childhood. A radical in politics, in touch with reformers of all evils, Herndon was Lincoln's political agent, and no man could have had a more devoted or capable one.

CHAPTER III

ECLIPSE : 1846 – 1854

Candidate for Congress – the Mexican War – in Congress – Alexander Stephens – the search for a job – return to the Bar

LINCOLN was resolved in 1846 to insist on the principle of rotation in his own favour. His right to a turn in Congress was the basis of all his campaign, and it was accepted by the local Whigs. The campaign was fought on vague issues – on the tariff and on the necessity of federal grants for local public works, for " internal improvements," which the Democratic president, Polk, had refused to sanction. There was nothing about the crisis which was leading to war with Mexico. Illinois was in favour of the war. Volunteers flocked to join the army that was to capture " the Halls of Montezuma," among them being Lincoln's predecessor in Congress, Hardin, and by the spring of 1847, when Lincoln arrived in Washington, the war and its victories had produced problems far more exciting than the tariff and than internal improvements. The conquests from Mexico revived the old slavery controversy and the still older sectional controversy. Polk had compromised the Oregon question by dividing the disputed territory with Britain, leaving to her the southern part of what is now British Columbia. To many in the North this seemed a betrayal, and such suspicions made opposition to annexation of Mexican territory, that might be turned into

slave states, all the keener. Opposition to Polk's
policy was not confined to enemies of slavery or
of " southern aggression," for the national Whig
party, while supporting the war once it was begun,
continued to assail the President's diplomacy,
which, they said, had forced war on Mexico and
had covered up the crime by disgraceful lying.
Lincoln threw himself into the party conflict with
what proved to be an indiscreet zeal. He harassed
the Democrats, demanding what " spot " of
American territory had been invaded by Mexico,
and thus impugned Polk's good faith. The
" spot " resolution made no great impression in
Congress or out of it, except in Illinois – and there
it made a bad one. Lincoln was accused of
betraying his country and his constituents who
were fighting for that country. While *he* was
slandering the President and giving aid and comfort to the enemy, his predecessor, Hardin, was
fighting and dying in Mexico ! In Congress,
Lincoln was merely an obtrusive new member.
He was most closely associated with a small group
of fighting Whigs, " the young Indians," a group
whose most remarkable member was the Geor-
gian, Alexander Stephens, deeply admired by
Lincoln for his courage and ability, destined to a
great congressional career, and, as Vice-President
of the Confederate States of America, destined to
cross Lincoln's path again at a fateful moment in
the history of the nation and of both men. Like
Hardin, Lincoln had announced he would not
run again, a promise he regretted, but which was
of little moment, since his successor as Whig candidate was beaten, largely because of the unpopu-
larity which Lincoln's " unpatriotic " conduct

had brought upon his party. The local defeat
was covered up, for the moment, in national victory. The Whigs, in 1848 as in 1840, abandoned
their great leaders, refused to nominate either
Clay or Webster, and nominated, instead, the
chief military hero of the Mexican war, Zachary
Taylor. No one knew what political opinions
General Taylor possessed ; the best authorities
did not think he had any ; but to astute politicians
that was an advantage. Lincoln shared this
opinion. Victory was what counted, and victory
was probable with Taylor, who might well have
said :

> " *Ez to my princerples, I glory*
> *In hevin' nothin' o' the sort ;*
> *I ain't a Wig, I ain't a Tory,*
> *I'm jest a candidate in short.*"

There were many Whigs, however, who did not
share Lincoln's plastic views. The party, they
thought, could only make itself ridiculous by
running a candidate who had, as his only claim
to fame, victories in a war which the party had
denounced as unnecessary and unjust. If the war
had been a slave-owners' conspiracy, how could
Whigs be asked to vote for a candidate who was a
large slave-holder ? There was grave danger
that many Whigs, especially in New England,
would either refuse to vote or would join a new
party that had just been launched. The " Free
Soil " party was formed by disgruntled Democrats who regarded the jettisoning of Van Buren
in 1844 as party treason, and were resolved to pay
in their own coin the Southern Democrats who
had " put over " Polk. To them were joined

CL

many Whigs who were increasingly hostile to slavery extension, and who regarded the Mexican war as a war for new slave territories. The Free Soil party candidates, taken together, were formidable. Van Buren was nominated for the Presidency ; he would win many Democrats ; Charles Francis Adams was nominated for the Vice-Presidency, and his name was a programme in itself. His father, John Quincy Adams, after being President, had entered the House of Representatives and had fought there the attempts of the South to suppress the freedom of petition against slavery. He had died in the Capitol while Lincoln was a member, and the association of Van Buren and Adams was an indication of how dangerous the temper of the North was growing, how the slavery issue was cutting across party lines. It was the business of the Whigs to see that the Free Soil party did more harm to the Democrats than to themselves. It was to this end that Lincoln made his first public speeches outside Illinois. He spoke in Massachusetts, with ability but in the usual campaign style ; he got a little local notice, but that was all. The estimate his party put on his services was shown by the job he was offered when Taylor was duly elected. He hoped to be Commissioner of the Land Office ; the job was given to a man who had done less hack work for the party than Lincoln. There was talk of making him Governor of Oregon Territory, but it came to nothing. The only definite offer made was that of Secretary of the Oregon Territory, an office whose importance is sufficiently indicated by the fact that the corresponding job in Nevada was given, twelve years later, to

Mark Twain's feather-brained elder brother, Orion
Clemens. Lincoln had alienated a powerful
section of his party at home. The Whigs of
Illinois, always weak, were now feeble indeed,
and his excessively loyal services to the national
party had been recompensed by an offer that was
an insult. He was nearly forty, and a career of
indefatigable political activity, pursued by an
able man with all the skill he could command in
the tricks of the trade, had ended in complete
defeat. There was nothing for it but to return
to Springfield. " He dripped melancholy " –
so one of Lincoln's closest friends described him
in the years which followed his political eclipse.
That, in itself, was enough to depress so ambitious
a man as Lincoln, for it forced him back to the
drudgery of the Bar, although his passion for
politics was as great as ever, and it forced him
back to life with Mrs. Lincoln in Springfield. She
was even more ambitious than her husband, and
her disappointment took shape, not in melancholy, but in temper. " She was a hellion," said
one friend of Lincoln's. She had little fitness for
home-making ; she found it hard to keep servants,
and missed the comfort of having slaves who could
not leave her. She spent money on dress and
show, but little on food. Fortunately, Lincoln
was ascetic, not from principle but from lack of
appetite ; he cared not at all what he ate, and
neither smoked nor drank. What pleasures he
had were the pleasures of sociability, of talk, or of
reading and brooding. He was indifferent to
appearances to a degree astonishing even on the
frontier ; he never had more than half of his
suspenders (braces) in operation, and in default of

buttons he occasionally used pegs. There were
few visitors to the Lincoln household, and, when
there were, Mrs. Lincoln might discover to her
horror that her husband had let them in in his
shirt-sleeves and slippers ! A son died and two
more were born as the Lincolns settled down to
the life of the little town, with its five thousand
inhabitants, already divided into the more and
less prosperous, but simple and unstratified compared with that great world which they had
glimpsed in Washington, that great world in
which young Stephen Douglas was beginning to
shine in the Senate as he had already shone in the
House of Representatives.

All dreams of office hidden, if not put away,
Lincoln turned to his old profession, which he
now loved little. He quickly regained his place
at the Bar, and his reputation grew ; he was an
excellent lawyer with a good case, a poor one
with a bad case. He was honest – notoriously so
– free from the pettier tricks of his trade, but not
the modern whimsical Saint Francis of legend,
going about doing good, careless of reward. He
appeared on both sides of most questions, even of
the slavery question, although he was notoriously
opposed to slavery. He argued for and against
rich clients. He lived up to the highest standards
of his profession, but not beyond them. For six
months of the year he was on the circuit, the only
lawyer of his own eminence who visited every
town. Thus he got to know hundreds of local
leading citizens in central Illinois, and they got
to know him, to know his wit, his wisdom, his
astonishing fits of abstraction when he voyaged
in strange seas of thought alone – thought of no

very cheering character, his sad, abstracted expression suggested. It was on the circuit that Lincoln was nearest happiness. There were the men who could tell him stories and who would listen to his ; there he got to know and understand the common man, juror or client ; the dirt and discomfort of the inns were of no account ; the long days riding across the empty prairie, the life of the courtroom, took him away from the melancholy house in Springfield. But Lincoln on the circuit did more than make a little money and keep away from home ; he made a very potent friend in the judge, David Davis. Judge Davis had a very high opinion of Lincoln ; he helped him in all his legal business and left him as deputy on the bench when the judge was called away on business. When the manœuvres which ended in Lincoln's nomination for the Presidency got under way, it was Davis, more than any other man, who brought them to a successful conclusion. Lincoln was not ungrateful, for he made Davis a Justice of the Supreme Court of the United States : in the dark days, Davis had had faith in him.

Slowly Lincoln acquired a modest competence, but he was extremely unbusinesslike in his methods, still leaving all book-keeping to his partner Herndon, keeping important papers in his hat, showing something of Thomas Lincoln's slackness. Although he could be eloquent and impassioned when really moved, his best work as a jury lawyer was in straightforward expositions to the jury, in which his knowledge of them and their knowledge of him counted. His statements of facts were wholly reliable, and, although not a

great lawyer, he was, if given time to prepare, a
sound one. Thus he did better in Illinois Supreme
Court appeals, when he could work up his case,
than in lower courts, where his slowness of mind
and lack of legal learning sometimes told against
him. His limitations as a lawyer were brought
home to him painfully in a case which was as
great a disappointment as his political failures.
In a very important patent case between the
McCormick Reaper Company and alleged in-
fringers of Cyrus McCormick's patents, the
defendants thought it advisable to have a local
lawyer, and Lincoln was suggested. It was the
most important litigation in which he had been
engaged, and he prepared for it with great care ;
the trip to Cincinnati for this case was a sally out
of the confined world of Illinois. Two leading
lawyers were associated with Lincoln, George
Harding and Edwin Stanton, both Pennsylvania
men, who looked with astonishment and acute
disfavour on the odd frontier figure who met them
and with whom they were supposed to act. Both
agreed that Lincoln must be kept out of the case ;
he was not allowed to speak, and his laborious
argument was returned to him unread. Seven
years later Lincoln made that rude, ill-tempered,
and arrogant man, Edwin Stanton, his Secretary
of War. Excluded from the case, Lincoln at first
refused his fee, but, when it was offered a second
time, took it. He was not normally averse to his
regular fee, and, on one occasion, sued for a fee
that many thought excessive and which was the
largest he ever received. As counsel for the
Illinois Central Railroad, he was one of a group
of lawyers who successfully defended that

corporation from an attempt made by a county
to tax it. For that service he demanded $5,000,
which the hard-pressed railroad had no means of
paying. Lincoln stuck to his guns, even taking
the long trip to New York to talk the matter over,
and at last got his money as the result of a friendly
suit – a victory of real importance, for it provided
him with some spare cash for his political " come-
back " of 1858. In another important case,
where the river transport interests and the river
towns, headed by St. Louis, fought the railway
interests, and so Chicago, Lincoln was on the
winning side, which was not only important from
the point of view of prestige, but made him
friends in Chicago. He had refused to settle
there, but he now was known, and favourably
known, in the fastest growing city in America –
the home of the great Senator Douglas.

If Lincoln was not always defending the widow
and the orphan, he was ready to do so – free, if
necessary. He defended the widow of a soldier
who was being cheated by a pension agent, his
notes for the case ending with the words, " *Skin
def't.*" He did skin him, with great effect. In
another case, he defended the ne'er-do-well son
of an old friend. " Duff " Armstrong was charged
with murder arising out of a drunken brawl near
a camp meeting. Armstrong's mother appealed
to Lincoln to save the son of his old friend of New
Salem days, Jack Armstrong. Lincoln agreed,
and, despite all the evidence, got young Armstrong off. It was in this case that Lincoln
played the famous almanac trick, inducing a
witness to commit himself as to the position of
the moon at the moment of the murder and then

producing an almanac which contradicted the witness. In improved versions of this story, Lincoln produces the almanac of the year before ! In any case, it was not the almanac that did the trick, but Lincoln's appeal to the soft hearts of the jury. The sorrow of the widowed mother if she lost her son was stressed with all Lincoln's command of pathos ; he evoked the memory of his dead friend, and, with tears streaming down his face, asked for an acquittal. He got it by this masterpiece of sentimental appeal, a type of legal triumph apparently rarer in America then than now.

Lincoln had no real reason to be discontented with his professional position. He was not a great national figure in law, any more than he was in politics, but he ranked a good deal higher in local legal than in local political circles. Many men who would never vote for him liked him and trusted him, and were willing to employ him. Unlike most of his contemporaries, unlike most Americans, Lincoln had no interest in speculation. Judge Davis and Senator Douglas and all the other leading citizens of the state might buy lands and stocks and become rich ; Lincoln simply put by a little money. He did not despise money ; but it excited no cupidity in him and he never judged men by their money or lack of it. He had plenty of ambition, but no greed and no envy. Yet he was an unhappy man. His home life was drab at best, intolerable at worst. He was very patient with Mrs. Lincoln, loved her in a fashion, and delighted in his children, whom he spoiled ; especially did he allow complete freedom to his eldest son, Robert, and protect him from the world, as he was later to protect him from the war. His own family were still shiftless poor whites. Lincoln did not think he owed his father much : he paid his debts, he wanted him looked after, but he did not want him in Springfield. Even if Lincoln had been a model of filial piety, Mrs. Lincoln would not have tolerated her worthless father-in-law in the house. When his father lay dying, Lincoln avoided going to see him, and the death was no great sorrow. He owed his father nothing but life, and that was a pretty poor gift at best. Death was no great tragedy, and Lincoln's mind ran on it ; his taste in literature was ribald or morbid and his favourite poem was Knox's string of platitudes, of which the first line has survived oblivion because Lincoln was never tired of quoting it : " Oh, why should the spirit of mortal be proud ? " Lincoln, at any rate, had no reason to be proud. He had been given a glimpse of the great world of politics in which Douglas shone and in which even his old enemy Shields had managed to enter the Senate on the strength of a wound won in the Mexican war. He had seen the rising lawyers, agents, and allies of the great business interests who were moving west every year, transforming the frontier into the model of an industrial and acquisitive society, creating a world in which Abraham Lincoln, at times, seemed as out of place as old Tom Lincoln had been when the hunter gave way to the farmer. Edwin Stanton and another acquaintance, Captain George McClellan, who had left the army to rescue the Illinois Central Railroad from bankruptcy, might succeed in that world, but Lincoln was too old to change. The legacy of the Mexican war had been a sectional conflict that almost tore the Union apart. The South had threatened secession as the admission of California as a free state threatened to upset the sectional balance in the Senate. Laborious negotiations had ended in the " Compromise of 1850," which both parties had accepted, a compromise full of seeds of future trouble, for it made it easier to recover fugitive slaves, and Mrs. Stowe was soon to make millions of hearts beat with Eliza crossing the ice to a freedom which the Fugitive Slave Act would deny her. It abolished the slave-trade in the District of Columbia (Washington), thus ending a scandal which Lincoln had attacked when in Congress. It left open the question of slavery extension, but it was generally assumed that the Missouri Compromise of 1820 still stood – that no slave territories should be formed north of 36° 30'. In all the exciting conflicts of these years Lincoln had no part. With the death of Webster, Clay, and Calhoun, the way was clear for new men : for Senator Seward of New York, who was the closest adviser of President Taylor ; for Senators Sumner of Massachusetts and Chase of Ohio, who called themselves " Free Democrats " and who saw the dread hand of the slavocracy everywhere ; for Senator Jefferson Davis of Mississippi, son-in-law of General Taylor, like his father-in-law a hero of the Mexican war, now the hope of southern Democrats ; and, outshining them all, if not in ability, in power to win and hold the multitudes, Senator Douglas of Illinois.

The Whig victory of 1848 was as barren as their victory of 1840 ; again their President died, and

was succeeded by an upright but unexciting
politician, Millard Fillmore. When election year
came round in 1852, there was a last despairing
attempt to pull off another Presidential victory by
nominating the rival hero of the Mexican war,
General Winfield Scott ; but the Whig game was
up. Scott was handsomely beaten by a much
inferior general, but superior politician, Franklin
Pierce, and the party to which Lincoln had given
so much of his life was dead.

CHAPTER IV

CRISIS : 1854–1858

Stephen Douglas and the Nebraska Bill – the Republican Party –
Lincoln and slavery – the senatorial nomination – " bleeding
Kansas " – the election of 1856 – the Dred Scott decision.

THIS painful truth was emphasised by the rise into
dominance in national politics of Lincoln's old
friend and rival, Stephen Douglas ; but, unknown
to both men, the stage was being set for a recast-
ing of the scene which was to bring Lincoln back
into politics. The origins of this change were
varied, but not extraordinary. Douglas was the
leader of the movement for western expansion ;
that movement was held up by the existence,
across the Missouri, of lands occupied only by
Indians and a few squatters. To open these lands
to regular settlement by organising them as a
territory – that is, by giving them local home
rule, preliminary to admission as a state – was
an urgent task for a politician with Douglas's
western plans. Through these lands he (and
many others) hoped to run that transcontinental
railway of which men had dreamed since the con-
quest of California. Local politics in Iowa made
it advisable to split the territory, which was
divided into a northern half (Nebraska) and a
southern half (Kansas). Kansas lay due west of
Missouri, and Douglas, in the difficult task of
collecting votes to put the scheme through, had
reason to conciliate the powerful Senator Atchison, who was fighting the veteran Benton for

control of that state. By declaring that the Missouri Compromise of 1820 had been repealed by the Compromise of 1850, it was possible to help Atchison and also to get votes for the northern railway scheme, instead of the more southern route favoured by the Secretary of War, Jefferson Davis. Thus, as an incident to that complicated strategy of sections which was always involved in such territorial questions, the chairman of the Senate Committee on Territories – that is, Douglas – introduced a Bill allowing the settlers in the new territories to vote for the introduction of slavery should they desire it. This option in fact only applied to the southern half of the territory, to Kansas ; but the great agitation which sprang up began while the name Nebraska was still applied to the whole area west of the Missouri. In its final form, the Nebraska Bill was reported to the Senate on January 23rd, 1854, but on the 19th Senators Sumner of Massachusetts and Chase of Ohio had issued their manifesto, *The Appeal of the Independent Democrats in Congress to the People of the United States*. In this manifesto, what Douglas had regarded as a bold but necessary piece of sectional strategy, which it was, appeared as a move in the never-ending campaign of the aggressive slavocracy to extend the area of the " peculiar institution." The manifesto was a call to arms.

The version sent out by Chase and Sumner had the merit of plausibility. There was a market in the country for any politician who could find a ground on which to rally opposition to the dominant Democrats. The disconsolate Whigs and the still angry " Free-Soilers " of 1848 rallied at once to the " Anti-Nebraska " cause, but more ominous was the number of orthodox Democrats who defied President Pierce and voted against the Bill. The Cave of Adullam, which Chase and Sumner had run with little success for years, was now full to overflowing. It was noted, as a sign of the times, that Senator Seward of New York, the most important survivor of the derelict Whig party, had joined in the clamour, and Seward was not merely an eloquent, he was an astute and influential man. Douglas was undaunted. He had not failed to allow for the risks of the complicated transaction he had carried through, but the fury of the storm was more than any politician could have foreseen. Party discipline forced the Bill through, and the first round was Douglas's. But 1854 was an election year ; and the five months that followed the enactment of the Bill in May were to see an immense change in the political landscape and in the life and prospects of Lincoln.

The decay of the Whig and the schism in the Democratic party opened the way for two new organisations, one destined to brief life, one to a great history. The first of these was the " Know-Nothings," or, to give it its official title, The American Party. The Know-Nothings[1] were defenders of Americanism and Protestantism, both menaced by the flood of immigrants from Ireland and Germany which had begun to pour into America in the late 'forties. Their social habits and their economic competition produced

[1] The Know-Nothings were a secret society whose members were instructed to profess ignorance of the party in public. This secrecy gave them their nickname, and added, for the moment, to the terror they inspired among cautious politicians.

the reactions with which modern Germany and, a few years ago, those parts of the United States ruled by the Ku Klux Klan, have made the world familiar. The new party won sweeping successes ; it attracted to its ranks very many old Whigs, but its permanent importance lies in the seed-bed it provided for the party into which the Anti-Nebraska Democrats and Whigs were merging. The Republican party, which was born in 1854 as a result of the campaign against Douglas, took the old name of the Jeffersonian party. The Democrats professed to be the spiritual heirs of Jefferson ; the new party denied the title of the Democrats to the assets of the Jeffersonian name. The name Republican was non-committal, and it eased things for the seceding Democrats. For the moment, the chief plank of the party was the repeal of the Missouri Compromise and inflexible resistance to the aggression of the " Slave Power." The adherents of the new party believed in the conspiracy theory, believed that Douglas was the tool, or willing ally, of the slave-holding oligarchs, and were resolved to punish all the adherents of the " Little Giant " who had betrayed the North.

In Illinois, the chief of these adherents who was due to come up for judgment was Senator Shields. In the passionate wave of feeling against Douglas, his junior colleague was sure to go down before the allies – the old Whigs, the active anti-slavery zealots, and the Democrats who had " bolted " their party. In this tangle Lincoln saw a chance to return to public life, and to do so dramatically, by entering the Senate. One obvious way to take the field would have been to join the Republicans, but this Lincoln resolutely refused to do. It was by no means certain which of the two new parties would survive, or if either of them would. Nor was it certain that Lincoln could carry with him his political assets, the trust and admiration of the old Whigs. Many eminent and many humble Whigs were averse to supporting the organised sectional organisation calling itself the Republican party. Some began to go over to the Democrats, who promised more safety for the union ; others joined the Know-Nothings, the more easily that Douglas professed to regard the Nebraska issue as settled and the opposition to Shields as being based on his Irish birth. All these dangers of precipitate action were plain to Lincoln : more astonishing, they were plain to his fiery partner, Herndon, who was himself one of the first Republican recruits, but who showed real skill in enabling Lincoln to evade the issue by escaping from Springfield before a meeting in which he would have had to say yea or nay.

But if Lincoln refused to take a stand on the immediate question of political tactics, he did take a stand, for the first time, on the great question underlying all the political manœuvres, underlying the high politics of Douglas and the low politics of the small towns of Illinois – the question of slavery.

Douglas, who had seen his way home from Washington lighted by the fires which were burning him in effigy, who had been shouted down in Chicago, whose greatest citizen he was, came to Springfield and made a speech there which showed how much fight he had in him yet and how great was his hold over the multitude. On

the next day Lincoln replied – a new Lincoln.
The able court lawyer, the astute political speaker
which Lincoln had shown himself to be, could
not have stood up to the " Little Giant," for
Douglas was a great man. But the Lincoln who
spoke on October 4th, 1854, revealed to his friends
(who had never suspected it), and perhaps to himself, that he too was a great man. He had none
of Douglas's oratorical energy ; his voice was
rasping, and he never took command of a meeting, hostile or friendly, as did Douglas on in-
numerable occasions. But the speech which he
now delivered came from a man who had, at last,
found himself in the slavery controversy, as he
could never have found himself on questions of
tariffs or treasuries. Lincoln was not, and never
became, a master of detail, an administrator and
legislator like Douglas, but the question, as
Lincoln saw it, did not call for the legislator or
the administrator or the acute constitutional
lawyer. It called for the prophet and the man
of faith. Much of the speech was common form,
although the violent abuse and the repeated
charges of ill faith with which Chase and Sumner
salted their oratorical dishes were absent. But
the core of the question, so Lincoln asserted, lay
in the wrongness of slavery, and the wrongness of
slavery was so patent to all who were not blinded
by sophistry that its existence " deprives our
Republican example of its just influence in the
world ; enables the enemies of free institutions
to taunt us as hypocrites ; causes the real friends
of freedom to doubt our sincerity ; and especially
because it forces so many good men among ourselves into an open war with the very fundamental

DL

principles of civil liberty, criticising the Declaration of Independence, and insisting that there is no right principle of action but self-interest."

Criticising the Declaration of Independence ! It is difficult to convey the meaning of that phrase to Lincoln and to his audience. To him, and to them, the United States was unique in the world, not because of its wealth or power but because it was the vehicle of a great experiment, because the wealth and power of the Union were challenges to the old world which lived under feudalism, under absolute monarchy ; an old world which had recently seen the second French Republic end in the Second Empire, which had seen the crushing of Poland and Hungary and Ireland in the name of divine right or superior power and wisdom. Save for Switzerland and the unsatisfactory commonwealths of Latin America, there was no republic in the world but this, and the United States had been born with a certificate of birth which committed it to beliefs which it could only betray by committing moral suicide. To preserve and extend slavery, more and more Americans had become willing to commit that crime, to deny those truths which the Declaration had asserted to be self-evident. That was a wrong to the white American, and to the whole future of the world, greater even than the wrong done the ignorant black. In pursuit of sectional and personal ambitions, the party of Jefferson was willing to deny in deed, and too often in word, that " all men are created equal, that they are endowed by their creator with certain inalienable rights, that among these are life, liberty, and the pursuit of happiness." It was possible to hold

this dogma firmly and yet to regard slavery as a
necessary evil ; it was not possible to hold it and
to regard slavery as a good, as so many now did
in the South ; it was not possible to hold that
dogma and believe, with Douglas, that slavery
was a thing indifferent. " The spirit of seventy-
six[1] and the spirit of Nebraska are utter antagon-
isms ; and the former is rapidly being displaced
by the latter. Is there no danger to liberty itself
in discarding the earliest practice and first
precept of our ancient faith ? " To turn back the
tide, to re-adopt the Declaration, was the duty
of the American people ; if this national apostasy
was checked, not only would the Union be saved
but " we shall have so saved it as to make and
to keep it for ever worthy of the saving. We shall
have so saved it that the succeeding millions of
free, happy people, the world over, shall rise up
and call us blessed to the latest generations."

It is difficult, to-day, to recapture that faith in
political arrangements that inspired Lincoln, and
which he managed to communicate to others.
The illusions of another generation are transparent enough, but it is important for the life of
Lincoln to realise that democracy was no illusion
for him, but a way of liberation which he himself
had trodden and which he saw being closed to
weak and feeble men – now to black men, but
how soon to white ?

The anti-Douglas forces carried the state legislature which was to elect a successor to Shields.
Would they elect Lincoln ? Lincoln's restless
ambition was fully awake, if it had ever been

[1] 1776, the year of Declaration and of the birth of the United
States.

asleep and not merely numbed by despair. He
hoped to be the choice of the allies and, to leave
the coast clear, he resigned from the legislature
to which he had been elected. But the political
situation, combined with a bad blunder of his
own, disappointed him. He neglected the by-
election to replace him in the legislature, and a
Douglas man was chosen – in Lincoln's own
county ! More important was the reluctance of
the extreme anti-slavery forces to give resolute
support to one who had been as cautious as
Lincoln in his dealings with the new party. The
victor was Lyman Trumbull, a bolting Democrat,
and Lincoln was not only beaten, he was humili-
ated, for he had not withdrawn early enough to
acquire much merit, and, on the other hand, his
Whig partisans were angered to a degree that
boded ill for the alliance. It was the greatest blow
of Lincoln's political career ; and it was a greater
blow to Mary Lincoln even than to her husband.
She had been an eager spectator of the fight in
the legislature, and the destruction of her hopes
was more than her uneasy temper could bear.
Mrs. Trumbull was her old schoolgirl friend,
Julia Jayne, but, while Lincoln remained on good
terms with the victor, Mrs. Lincoln never spoke
to Mrs. Trumbull again.

The defeat of Lincoln's senatorial ambitions
did not lead to the passivity which he had adopted
after the collapse of the Whigs. The hastily
assembled " Anti-Nebraska " alliance was holding together. Lincoln still avoided too open
fellowship with the Republicans, but, as the wave
of popular indignation that had been behind the
campaign of 1854 died down, events in Kansas

came to the rescue. The application of the doctrine of " popular sovereignty " in Kansas was
not proving as easy as Douglas had thought.
Settlers and pseudo-settlers crossed from Missouri
to help to turn Kansas into a slave territory.
Their activities, reported and exaggerated in the
North, provoked organised and armed immigration from the free states. The contest in Kansas
thus took not only the form of disputed elections
and rival constitutions but of miniature civil war.
The new territory became notorious as " Bleeding
Kansas," and, as long as Kansas bled, the new
party had an effective talking-point. Lincoln did
not believe all the stories that came out of Kansas ;
he was not a credulous man, and he had better
information from friends in the territory than
could be got from a northern press, fed, by not too
scrupulous agitators, with atrocity – stories that
were, if not quite baseless, highly spiced.

There was enough dirty work on both sides for
the partisan, North and South, to glut his appetite for moral indignation, but Lincoln's mind was
not capable of the infallible divination of moral
qualities that marked a Sumner. Yet he saw in
the Kansas struggle, even when all allowance
was made for innocent and for not so innocent
fiction, enough evidence of the failure of the
Douglas doctrine. Whatever else it had done,
it had not ended the slavery controversy, and
Lincoln began to share with others his pessimism
as to the way in which that ever-living controversy would end. " Can we as a nation continue
together permanently – for ever – half slave and
half free ? " He was to ask that question, publicly
and with immense effect, a little later.

The Kansas struggle went on, in Kansas and in Washington ; it paid the opposition to keep it alive until election year, and, in any case, the longer the struggle lasted, the less likely was Kansas to go over to slavery. A territory as disturbed as this was no place for a southern planter, no matter how zealous for the cause, to take slaves worth fifteen hundred dollars apiece, and the territorial government set up by the slavery party recognised this by the ferocious laws it passed to punish persons aiding slaves to escape. At the best, with a friendly local and federal government, slavery in Kansas would be a tender plant. But the Kansas atrocities were now given dramatic force by the Sumner affair. Sumner, in a long, violent, and, to-day, quite unreadable speech called " The Crime Against Kansas," had attacked Senator Butler and his state, South Carolina, with that ill-mannered invective in which he specialised and indulged with a freedom possible only to the righteous. A nephew of the Senator, Congressman Preston Brooks, made an assault on Sumner in the Senate chamber, beating him unconscious with a heavy stick. The scandal was immense, in the North and in Europe. Classically minded men remembered the ominous precedent of the murder of the elder Gracchus from which came civil war and the death of the Roman republic. In the South, Brooks was a hero.

It was the year of a Presidential election ; the good luck that had attended the Republicans had not failed them. The atrocities that had been reported in Kansas now became credible ; if an assault which, it was believed, had crippled

Sumner for life, and would have killed a man of
less robust physique, could occur in the Senate,
what was going on in Kansas ? What was
going on was an atrocity far worse than
anything yet committed – the massacre of
southern settlers by the murderous northern
fanatic John Brown but that was not yet
generally known and the Republican party had
abundant ammunition. It had won over, in 1855,
the most famous of the younger Whigs, Senator
Seward of New York, and, with him, the much
admired state machine run by Thurlow Weed ; but
Lincoln still held aloof. The party summoned
a convention for June, and its prospects were
brightened by a split in the Know-Nothing ranks,
a split due to the emergence of the Kansas question
as a rival to the Pope as a topic of party eloquence.

It was increasingly likely that the Republicans,
not the Know-Nothings, would be the residuary
legatees of the Whigs. Yet not until May 1856
did Lincoln finally join the party which was to
make him President. Lincoln was chosen for the
honorary office of Presidential elector on the ticket
of the " Anti-Nebraska " party, as the fears of the
timid still insisted the Republicans should be
called, and at Peoria, and again at Bloomington,
he sounded the party " key-note," and did it
with astonishing effect. His oratory, limpid,
passionate, and elevated, which was his great and
recently discovered asset, impressed the rank and
file – and the leaders too. After Bloomington,
when the great meeting had been swept off its
feet, a friend first suggested to Lincoln that he
might be President. It seemed absurd, but men
who knew him well believed that Lincoln listened.

When the Republican national convention met, over a hundred votes were cast for Lincoln for the Vice-Presidential nomination. Politicians all over the country learned that, in Illinois, Lincoln was more than an obscure ex-Congressman ; Lincoln learned that he had more fame than he had suspected. From that year on, the Presidency was the object of his ambition – not vaguely, but definitely. He had never undervalued himself, and he came more and more to believe that others could see his qualities too.

But the new party seemed in danger of not surviving the election. It nominated as Presidential candidate John C. Frémont ; its slogan was, " Free soil, free men, and Frémont." The candidate was famous as an explorer, as the " conqueror of California," and he had made a romantic runaway match with Jessie Benton, daughter of the veteran Senator who had been a friend of Andrew Jackson when the Democratic party *was* democratic ; although Benton opposed his son-in-law, the connection was an asset. There was plenty to appeal to the voter in the candidate and the platform, but the zeal of the Republicans alarmed the safe business men, who had had no party of their own since the Whigs died. Most of them preferred the veteran Buchanan to the flamboyant Frémont. The Democratic candidate was above all "safe"; that was why he, and not Douglas, had been chosen, and the support he got from " the good, the wise, and the rich " showed that the Democrats had calculated well. Buchanan won the election ; more, he carried Sangamon county, and in Lincoln's own bailiwick, Frémont ran behind not only Buchanan, but even Fillmore who was the Know-Nothing candidate. It was evident that Lincoln had not carried over with him enough of the voting strength of the Whigs to make his position in the Republican ranks secure.

The position of the new party was now improved by one of the strokes of luck which favoured it all through its delicate childhood. President Buchanan, in his inaugural speech, referred to the imminent decision of the Supreme Court in the case of Scott *v.* Sanford as a welcome means of ending the endless controversy – and he called on all good citizens to obey the court.

The case arose out of a claim to freedom advanced by a negro, Dred Scott, who had been taken by his master into what is now the state of Minnesota, at that time part of a territory free under the Missouri Compromise. The court dismissed the case on technical grounds of jurisdiction, but went on to say that, in any case, the Missouri Compromise was unconstitutional, that Congress had no power to prohibit slavery in any territory. This decision cut the ground from under both the Republican and the Douglas programmes. We now know that, if there was any collusion or conspiracy in the case, it was on the other side, but it was easy in 1857 to represent the decision as another crime of the "Slave Power."

To complicate the situation the panic of 1857 burst on the country. The American elector, then as now, blamed the party in power for bad times, and the financial pressure was especially severe in a rapidly growing state like Illinois. The Republicans saw a chance to attack the Buchanan administration from a new angle. The United States was under a low tariff régime, and the old Whigs who had become Republicans began to preach their panacea, a high tariff, which would have the special value of damaging President Buchanan in his own state ; for Pennsylvania was more and more the centre of heavy industry, and powerful interests could be given sound business reasons for supporting the Republicans, no matter how dangerous and revolutionary their constitutional doctrines might be.

CHAPTER V

THE OPPONENT OF DOUGLAS : 1858–1860

The Lecompton Constitution – Douglas v. Buchanan – Lincoln as candidate – " A House divided " – the Lincoln-Douglas debates.

THERE were fairly good reasons for taking an optimistic view of Republican prospects when the arrival of the Kansas constitution in Washington presented the party leaders with an entirely new set of possible moves. The constitution, which was now submitted to Congress for ratification, had been adopted by the pro-slavery faction in Kansas at their capital, Lecompton. As the " Lecompton Constitution " it was soon famous. It represented the attempt of the southern party in the territory to save something out of the wreck of pro-slavery hopes, for it had become evident that hopes of a permanent addition of Kansas to the ranks of slave states were vain. As wise men in the South had seen (and as Douglas himself thought), there was nothing to be got in Kansas but shadowy satisfaction for *amour propre*. But wise men had been at an increasing discount in the South, and the conduct of the southern party in Kansas was designed to protect the property rights of the few slave-holders in Kansas and to attempt to secure the election of two Senators from what would be nominally a slave state. It was a pure question of prestige, for the majority against slavery in Kansas was large and daily growing larger, and, once admitted, as a state, Kansas was free to abolish slavery at once, with a complete legal security which the Dred Scott decision denied to a territory. The constitution produced did pay some homage to " popular sovereignty," since it allowed the settlers of Kansas to vote on the question of slavery. But it did not allow them to vote on the question of the constitution *apart from slavery*, and, when this aspect of the case came to Douglas's attention, he had to decide what should be his attitude. The President, and the leading members of his party, accepted the Lecompton Constitution as a convenient way of ending a tiresome controversy that had now lasted four years. The United States had other things to worry about, and, with the admission of Kansas, might be given a chance to look after them. The new constitution might, it was to be hoped, complete the pacifying work of the Dred Scott decision. These hopes were not unreasonable. The realisation of them would have been highly damaging to the Republicans, for their political life had begun with the Kansas controversy and might end with it. True, there was plenty of material for abuse in the unrepresentative character of the convention, and the Free Soilers' boycott of the elections had not been unconnected with the need for having something to complain about ; but if Kansas were admitted, the Republican postmortem could not last for ever and the Democrats would have won a game, perhaps the rubber.

Douglas shattered these hopes ; the situation was, of course, as clear to him as to Buchanan, and the risks Douglas took were so obvious and so great that all sorts of fantastic explanations were

invented to account for his course of action. Had
Douglas been the mere *condottiere* of politics he
was represented to be, devoid of scruple and
principle, slave of exorbitant ambition, his refusal
to agree with Buchanan, and the consequent
postponement of the funeral of the Kansas question, would, indeed, be inexplicable. But
Douglas's pride was not mere insolence, with no
ballast of principle. He had taken a great risk
for himself, and for his party, in introducing the
Kansas-Nebraska Bill ; he had done so, assuring
the whole nation that he had no desire to aid or
hinder slavery, that he was merely putting into
effect the old Democratic doctrine of local home
rule. Now he saw his promises being falsified by
the action of the Lecompton party in Kansas and
by the hasty acceptance of their handiwork by the
official head of the party, President Buchanan.

Douglas had no illusions about the tired old
man he had put into the White House, or any
doubts that there was a division of authority in
the Democratic party between the real and the
nominal ruler. When it was obvious that the
President was determined to exercise all his
formal authority, Douglas was furious. " By
God, sir, I made Mr. James Buchanan, and by
God, sir, I will unmake him." The President
was very much on his dignity, and when, at an
interview, Douglas refused finally to follow the
presidential lead, Buchanan attempted to cow
him by recalling the dire fate of eminent Democrats who had revolted against Buchanan's old
chief, President Jackson. But Douglas was not
scared by these threats from this " sheep in
sheep's clothing," to borrow a phrase from a later

age and another country. The quarrel between
Douglas and the administration was, indeed,
good news for the opposition, and the temptation
to make the breach too wide to be recrossed
assailed many Republicans, especially if the
consequences of the breach were not dangerous
to any personal ambitions.

Douglas was still the most powerful man in
politics, for if the Democratic Senators and Representatives had obeyed the party whip, the rank-
and-file Democrats had not. Douglas developed
astonishing strength. Obviously he was an ally
worth having ; the Republican defeat of 1856 had
chilled the hopes of many party members, and
they were willing to back Douglas against
Buchanan, or, at any rate, were willing to leave
him a free field in the contest which was looming
before him – his campaign for re-election to the
Senate in 1858. In Illinois, despite rigorous
pressure from the administration, despite the
dismissal of all federal office-holders who refused
to come out for the President instead of for the
Senator, Douglas had shown that his hold on his
party was as strong as ever. Not all Douglas's
followers were very clear why he had broken
with the President, but that he had was enough
for *them*. It would be easy, then, to make the
Illinois contest one in which the administration
would be forced to fight a battle in which, if the
Republicans backed Douglas or did not oppose
him, the government of the aggressive slavocracy
would be doomed to ignominious defeat. The
logic of events might even force Douglas into the
Republican camp. If that came about, victory
in 1860 was certain. So thought Horace Greeley,

and so wrote Greeley in that weekly edition of the
New York Tribune which was a fifth gospel to
thousands of Illinois farmers. To Republicans in
the East, in New York, in Boston, the wisdom and
prudence of this course of action seemed unques-
tionable, and there was a good deal of indignation
when it was discovered that Illinois was not
going to take the advice volunteered, but was
going to fight Douglas – fight him because he
" could not be trusted," and because the Republican nomination was the rightful property of
Abraham Lincoln ! In the East, such conduct
was inexcusable ; it was the sacrificing of the real
interests of the party, and the cause, to the vested
interests of an obscure prairie politician whose
chief claim to be a Senator in 1858 was that he
had failed to become one in 1854.

To Lincoln, to the passionate Herndon, Greeley
and his like were traitors to the party, and self-
righteous posers who were generous with other
people's property – the Republican nomination
in 1858. That nomination was now very valuable
indeed. Douglas might have captured the local
Democratic machine, but every federal official,
every land-agent, every postmaster, was his
sworn enemy. Moreover, thousands of conservative Whigs, who had refused to follow Lincoln
into the Republican party in 1856, were ready to
support him now, since Douglas seemed as dangerous to peace and prosperity now as Frémont
had seemed then. That the Senator had become
the darling of eastern " Black Republicans " was
a good reason for turning against him and taking
the most effective measures to render him im-
potent. It was distressing that the only choice

was between Douglas and Lincoln, but, since there was so little to choose between their principles, there could be no doubt which of the two would be less dangerous to the administration, to peace, to the Union. Senator Lincoln would be another vote on the wrong side ; Senator Douglas would be a voice, the most potent voice in the country.

There was too much bitterness in western politics for Lincoln to have much reason to fear that he would lose many votes because of Douglas's transformation from an ally into an enemy of the South. In any case, he could afford to lose a few. The great wave of immigration had begun. Between 1850 and 1860, the population of Illinois more than doubled. Two-thirds of that increase came from immigration, almost all of it from the eastern states and from Europe – and most of that immigration was composed of recruits for the Republican party. Illinois had been originally settled by southerners like Lincoln himself. The lower counties along the Mississippi, " Egypt " were still hostile to all " nigger lovers," full of old line Whigs and rock-ribbed Democrats who would never vote for a Republican, but the northern and eastern parts of the state were equally solid for the new party.

Lincoln had tried from the beginning to make the Republican party (even before he formally joined it) a party which would not repel immigrants. He had tried to repress tendencies to Know-Nothingism, always strong in the old Whig section. The same moral enthusiasm that had rallied the Protestant Churches against slavery, and which had been one of the main assets of the

Republican party, had also manifested itself in a campaign for prohibition. But it was hopeless to ask Germans and Irish to join a party which attacked slavery as an evil and yet proposed to deprive " the working man of his refreshment." Most of the Irish and many of the Germans were Catholics, already suspicious of the clerical allies of the Republicans ; to allow them to suspect that in voting against Douglas they would be voting against " liquor " was too dangerous to be risked. But Lincoln's tact was not put to the test. The passion for general reform that had assailed the Republicans in the first two years of their party life was dying down. One great cause was enough, and, for the moment, that was the defeat of Douglas – by fair means or by politics.

There was, for a moment, fear in the Lincoln camp that their own candidate might be jockeyed out of his rights by the astute Mayor of Chicago, " Long John Wentworth " ; and, to avoid any knavish tricks, it was decided to make the election of Lincoln as Senator part of the official party programme to be adopted when the state convention met at Springfield. This was an unprecedented honour, for, although all men knew that a vote for the state Democratic candidates for the legislature was a vote for Douglas as Senator, the fiction of a free choice by the legislature had been preserved. But the innovation was successful. If there had been a conspiracy to cheat Lincoln, it failed, and he was nominated. When Douglas learned who was to be his opponent, he told a friend that the Republicans had made the best choice they could ; that Lincoln would be a formidable opponent, " full of wit, facts, dates –

E1

and the best stump speaker, with his droll ways and dry jokes, in the West." The platform on which Lincoln was to run was a skilful piece of political carpentry. The Germans having been placated by making Gustave Koerner President of the Convention, it was not thought necessary to make any declaration in favour of tolerance such as had been made in 1856. There were plenty of Know-Nothings, who had voted for Fillmore in 1856, now looking for a home. The need for a high tariff, which was being preached in the East, was ignored here. There were vague generalities in abundance ; in short, a typical party platform.

Lincoln was an astute politician, and could have played up to the party platform with equally ingenious exhibitions of the arts of Mr. Facing-Both-Ways ; however, he was not only astute, as Douglas had said, but, as Douglas had added, he was honest. The time had come for candour, and, at eight o'clock in the evening of June 16th, 1858, Lincoln addressed the Convention in terms that must have surprised the members almost as much as they had surprised and scared most of the leaders who had been informed of what he was to say. Disregarding his usual custom, Lincoln read his speech. " If we could first know *where* we are, and whither we are tending, we could then better judge *what* to do, and *how* to do it. We are now far into the *fifth* year since a policy was initiated, with the *avowed* object, and *confident* promise, of putting an end to slavery agitation. Under the operation of that policy, that agitation has not only *not ceased* but has continually *augmented*. In *my* opinion it *will* not cease until a *crisis* shall have been reached and passed. A house divided against itself cannot stand. I believe this government cannot endure ; permanently half *slave* and half *free*. I do not expect the Union to be *dissolved* – I do not expect the house to fall – but I do expect it will cease to be divided. It will become *all* one thing, or *all* the other."[1] Slowly and with emphasis, Lincoln announced his thesis. The narrow question of the rights of the slave states to control of their own life, and the disputed claim to free access to the common territories, had been merged in a greater problem. Were the free states to be cajoled out of their rights under cover of law ? Were there not now apparent answers to the question, "Whither are we tending?" Was not the Dred Scott decision, like the Kansas-Nebraska Act, like the conduct of the administrations of President Pierce and of President Buchanan, a sign of a conspiracy, not merely to protect slavery where it had legal rights, but to extend it into the free states ? Were there not ambiguities in the wording both of the Kansas-Nebraska Act and of the Dred Scott decision which left the way open for an attack on freedom in Illinois and in the other free states ? It was impossible to *prove* a conspiracy, but " when we see a lot of framed timbers, different portions of which we know have been gotten out at different times and places and by different workmen – Stephen, Franklin, Roger and James, for instance[2] – and when we see these timbers joined together, and see they exactly make the frame of a house or a mill . . . in *such* a case we

---

[1] Italics Lincoln's.

[2] Stephen Douglas, Franklin Pierce, Roger Taney, James Buchanan.

find it impossible to not *believe* that Stephen and
Franklin and Roger and James all understood one
another from the beginning, and all worked upon
a common *plan* or *draft* drawn up before the first
lick was struck."

Lincoln's speech delighted his party and made
them even more confident than they had been.
There seemed, indeed, good reason for their
confidence. The strength shown by the party in
1856 had not been lost. If Douglas had got back
some deserters by his opposition to the Lecompton
Constitution, he had alienated a good deal of the
Whig support the Democrats had gained by their
conservatism two years before, and, more important, he had alienated the official Democrats. All
the pressure of the administration machine was
directed against him, and many vociferous
Republicans who denounced Douglas and Buchanan as fellow conspirators secretly combined
with Buchanan's agents to beat the rebel Senator.
Lincoln was able, truthfully, to deny any knowledge of these intrigues, although he relied on a
split in the Democratic party to elect him, and
talked the situation over with at least one Buchanan Democrat whose independent candidature
would help the Republicans. Now, as later, the
less creditable side of politics offended Lincoln,
who had to be content not to let his right hand
know what his left hand did. As his partner
Herndon put it, " [Lincoln] does not know the
details of how we get along. . . . That kind of
thing does not suit his tastes, nor does it suit me,
yet I am compelled to do it." It was not merely a
righteously indignant electorate that Douglas had
to face, but a great orator, a great debater – with

some of the most astute and least pedantic of Illinois politicians in the background. Douglas had no illusions about the task before him, but he threw himself into the combat with all his old vigour. Speaking from his hotel window in Chicago, he at once attacked Lincoln, as he was to continue to attack him again and again, as a mischief-maker whose " house divided " speech was an invitation to disunion, was an attack on local liberty, a call to a " war of sections, a war of the North against the South, of the Free States against the Slave States – a war of extermination to be continued relentlessly, until the one or the other shall be subdued and all the States shall either become free or become slave." With a shrewd hit at Republican dallyings with prohibition, Douglas asserted that on the Lincoln principle there would have to be prohibition everywhere or nowhere ; the Union would become " one consolidated empire." Not only did the Republicans assail the rights of the states ; their attacks on the Supreme Court over the Dred Scott decision were endangering " our rights, and our liberty, and our property." One last, and still more deadly charge was then launched : the Republicans were the party of racial equality, all this insistence on the rights of the black man was endangering the rights of the white man for whom and by whom the government was made. " Preserve the purity of our government as well as the purity of our race ; no amalgamation, political or otherwise, with inferior races ! " The audience in Chicago thought this a palpable hit ; even in the ranks of the Republicans, far more opposed slavery than loved the Negro. The laws of Illinois, if they gave the Negro formal freedom, were far from putting him on anything like terms of equality with the white man ; he was a subject, not a citizen. And if the appeal to race prejudice was effective in Chicago, it was to be far more effective in the central and southern parts of the state, the parts settled by southern immigrants like Lincoln, counties like Lincoln's own, cities like Springfield. Douglas had not only Chicago in mind but " Egypt," the lower counties, where the administration might hurt him most and where he intended that Lincoln should be forced to recant some of his rash words about slavery and the two races – or damn himself with the voters who were white before they were Democrats or Whigs or Republicans. Lincoln had sat behind Douglas while he spoke, and he answered him the next night. When he talked about the house divided, Lincoln had merely described the situation ; he had not expressed his own wishes, but he *did* wish that slavery should become extinct, for he thought it wrong – as the makers of the constitution had done. Slavery *was* a moral question, and the attempt to treat it as a mere matter of local regulation was the great error of Douglas. Nor was the scepticism Lincoln felt about the Dred Scott decision revolutionary. Despite the decision, he would, if he had the chance in Congress, vote to keep slavery out of a territory, for the court was not infallible, he had a right to refuse obedience to it " as a political rule." The court could change its mind, and " we mean to do what we can to have the Court decide the other way." Douglas's indifference to the principles of the Declaration of Independence was dangerous to white immigrants as well as to black men. " Let us discard all this quibbling about this man and the other man, this race and that race and the other race, being inferior, and therefore they must be placed in an inferior position. Let us discard all these things, and unite as one people throughout this land, until we shall once more stand up declaring that all men are created equal."

In the remaining months of the campaign, neither Lincoln nor Douglas added much to their Chicago speeches. Douglas continued to assail the alliance of the " Black Republicans " and the administration Democrats. He continued to assert that he had defended self-government in 1854 against the passions of the North ; now he was defending it against the passions of the South. He declared that Lincoln's attitude was incompatible with the peace of the Union and with the supremacy of the white race. Lincoln might say that he only meant to preserve for the Negro the right to " life, liberty, and the pursuit of happiness " asserted by the Declaration of Independence to be among the natural rights of every man, but what the Republicans were really after was shown by the spectacle of the Negro orator, Frederick Douglass, being driven in a carriage along with his white hostess and her daughter !

Lincoln denied an alliance with the Buchanan Democrats, while admitting pleasure that the enemy was divided against himself. He returned again and again to the charge of conspiracy, of which the Dred Scott decision was an example, a conspiracy which would not be completely successful until the right of the free states to exclude slavery had been destroyed, a conspiracy of which Douglas was an originator – or a dupe. Because Lincoln thought slavery wrong, he did not therefore want to marry a slave, nor did he think black men the equals in all things of white men, nor was he willing to have them made citizens or voters in Illinois.

The interest of the state and the country in the campaign reached its height when it became known that the candidates had agreed to take part in a series of seven joint debates. The joint debate was a widespread political device, but Douglas was at first reluctant to accept Lincoln's challenge. He had a very high respect for his opponent's ability, and, as he wrote to a friend, should Lincoln get the best of the debates, " I shall lose everything. Should I win, I shall gain but little." But the " Little Giant " had not the spirit that lies quiet under a challenge, and he had, in any case, to carry the battle to his enemies; so the arrangements were made. On four occasions Douglas was to begin the debate with an hour's speech, Lincoln to reply in an hour and a half, and Douglas to speak for a half-hour to close. For the other three meetings, Lincoln was to open and to close.

The contrast between the two gladiators was dramatic enough. Douglas was short and sturdy, Lincoln long and lean. Douglas's manner as a speaker was aggressive, the manner of a man who says, "I'm not arguing; I'm telling you." He had neither the talent nor the taste for jests and anecdotes : he appreciated those of his friend Abe Lincoln, but his own method of speaking was very practical : he saw a weak or a sore spot and he hammered at it, and opponents who thought this an easy trick of controversy found, when *they* tried it, that Douglas's counter-attack was even more formidable than his first offensive. A man of considerable wealth, gained from the practice of the law and successful land speculation, Douglas, after a period of dissipation, was now in excellent condition, smartly dressed and very much in appearance and manner the gentleman and statesman. He was a great man, he knew it, and he showed he knew it. He had married again, and the improvement in his habits was attributed to his beautiful wife, who came to aid him in the campaign – a doubtfully useful ally, for her beauty and her fashionable dress possibly, and her Catholicism certainly, did not go down well with the worn and drab pioneer women of Illinois. But Republicans might whisper that Douglas had gone over to the Scarlet Woman and that he drank as much as ever, the " Little Giant " could depend on a noisy, devoted, and, it was very soon discovered, disconcertingly numerous body of supporters.

Lincoln, with his ill-fitting ready-made clothes, which never gave him sleeves long enough, with his battered old top hat, his shabby bag, and his cotton umbrella, was not an impressive figure. His thin neck and small head were not yet hidden by the whiskers he grew after he was elected President ; his high voice, which friendly critics found silvery, and unfriendly ones shrill, was not to be compared with Douglas's powerful baritone. While Douglas travelled as a rule in a special train, with a cannon on board to fire salutes, Lincoln walked or rode or took the ordinary train or a special just as it happened to suit ; he even travelled with the Senator when that potentate's movements suited his. But in the sadly depressed Illinois of 1858, still sore after the economic collapse of 1857, the homeliness of " Honest Abe " was no handicap. Douglas was perhaps *too* great a man – practically a permanent resident of Washington, husband of an heiress, too friendly with railroads and the great – to understand or sympathise with the average citizen of a raw frontier commonwealth. The other great asset of Lincoln – his incomparable superiority as an orator when at the height of his powers, not only to Douglas, but to any living or dead American – was less widely appreciated ; for the new classical style that Lincoln had adopted was not oratory as the average man understood it, not rich and ornate, every line loaded with brass, in the manner of Sumner or Chase or Yancey. The people of Illinois knew that Lincoln was an honest man, a smart man (the two did not always go together then), but they did not know that he was a great man, nor did anything happen in the debates to show them that he was.

Like many other episodes of Lincoln's life, the debates with Douglas have been overladen with legend. Lincoln's nobility, his candour, his inspired foresight, have been contrasted with Douglas's low cunning, shameless evasions, downright dishonesty, his mastery of all the arts of sophistry, arts foiled by Lincoln's almost superhuman wisdom in an emergency fit to perplex maturest counsels. Few readers of the *Debates* who come to them without prepossessions, will find them worthy of their reputation, or discover much moral or

intellectual difference between Lincoln's share of
them and Douglas's. Both speakers were men of
great ability, trying to induce marginal voters to
support them. For the vast bulk of the faithful
on both sides, there were stereotyped arguments ;
the independent voters were to be courted and
convinced, by art and by craft. Both Lincoln
and Douglas had earlier reached greater heights of
eloquence, of courage, of candour, of cogency of
argument, than they did in the joint debates.
They said over again what they had said before,
they made a few new debating points, they catered
to the different sections of the state ; they fell at
times (Lincoln at least as often as Douglas) into
rather noisy abuse of each other's good faith ;
but, with one exception, the debates were debates
in the less edifying sense of the word. There was
no Socratic deliverance of the truth ; too often
that delicate child was stifled by sophistries, and,
when needs must, both debaters were admirable
sophists, each in his own characteristic way.

The one possible exception is the question which
Lincoln put to Douglas at the second debate, at
Freeport (August 27th, 1858). Douglas was fond
of ramming the Dred Scott decision down Republican throats, but the decision was almost as
indigestible for a Douglas Democrat as for a Republican, since the Douglas dogma of the right
of the people of a territory to vote slavery " up
or down " was denied by the majority opinion of
the Supreme Court. " Can the people of a United
States Territory, in any lawful way, against the
wish of any citizen of the United States, exclude
slavery from its limits prior to the formation of
a state constitution ? " So Lincoln put the

dilemma. " I answer emphatically, as Mr. Lincoln has heard me answer a hundred times from every stump in Illinois, that in my opinion the people of a territory can, by lawful means, exclude slavery from their limits prior to the formation of a state constitution. . . . It matters not what way the Supreme Court may hereafter decide as to the abstract question whether slavery may or may not go into a territory under the constitution ; the people have the lawful means to introduce it or to exclude it as they please, for the reason that slavery cannot exist a day or an hour anywhere, unless it is supported by local police regulations."

Douglas could have said nothing else, and Lincoln's skill in forcing him to commit himself was great enough, without all the trimmings which legend has since added to it. Lincoln was trying to drive a wedge between Douglas and conservative Democrats ; the question and answer at Freeport were helpful, since they were another tap, or even another blow, on that wedge. But the belief that until then no one had thought of any inconsistency between the Douglas views on squatter sovereignty and what the South and the Supreme Court held to be slave-holders' rights in the territories, gives very little credit to either Douglas or his enemies. No one ever denied that Douglas was able, and he had seen the danger long before Freeport and had dealt with it, as he dealt with it at Freeport, by pointing out that (as the case of Kansas had shown plainly enough to all the world) the bare legal right to hold slaves in a territory was of no use to anybody. The position taken at Freeport was the only one

Douglas could take, consistent with his support of popular sovereignty ; and, in opposing Buchanan over Lecompton, Douglas had burnt his boats so completely that any further damage he did to his reputation in the South was of no importance. Whether he would alienate enough conservative Democrats in Illinois to give Lincoln a chance, was what mattered in 1858, and it was not until two years later, when Lincoln was a candidate for the Presidency, that the legend was born, the legend according to which Lincoln deliberately threw away his chances of being elected in 1858 in order to force Douglas to alienate the South and thus ruin his chances for the Presidency in 1860 ! If any speech this autumn had presidential results in 1860, it was that delivered by Senator Seward of New York, the most eminent political figure in the nation after Douglas, the most likely Republican candidate for the presidential election of 1860. " It is," said he, " an irrepressible conflict between opposing and enduring forces, and it means that the United States must and will, sooner or later, become either entirely a slave-holding nation or entirely a free-labour nation." It was the " house divided doctrine," but for one American outside Illinois who paid any attention to what Lincoln had said, there were ten who listened to Seward – and among them were enough conservative or timid men to be alarmed, and to spread their alarm to party managers, who henceforward regarded Seward as dangerous and his candidacy as possibly fatal to the young party, which could not afford a repetition of the Frémont fiasco.

By the time Seward spoke, the campaign was

all but over and Douglas had turned a forlorn hope
into a triumph. The legislature had a small
Democratic majority, and, although the Republicans elected a governor and claimed a moral
victory, the achievement of Douglas dazzled most
spectators ; he had taken his political life in his
hands and had saved it. Outside the South, he
was the idol of the Democrats, and, compared
with him, the Buchanan administration had few
supporters and fewer friends. Lincoln had again
tasted defeat, after delusive hopes of victory. It
was a blow, but, as he afterwards remembered,
there was an omen of better things. " I ascer-
tained that we had lost the legislature and started
to go home. . . . My foot slipped out from under
me, knocking the other out of the way ; but I
recovered and said to myself, ' It's a slip and not
a fall.' "

Lincoln had some real reasons to be pleased ;
far less than if he had won, but still not altogether
fictitious consolations for his defeat. The fame of
Douglas had reflected on his opponent, whose
name, at least, was now familiar to readers and
voters all over the country. More people than
Stephen Douglas had now learned that Lincoln
was a man of remarkable ability, and the refusal
of Lincoln and his friends to allow Douglas a
walk-over had, perhaps, saved the Republican
party from a false step that might have been
fatal to it.

There was now a demand for Lincoln as a
speaker outside his own state ; and a place for
him in his party, if not beside Seward and Chase,
at least among the second-raters – and being
a second-rater in American politics was a help,

not a hindrance, if one wanted to be President. No first-rater since Jackson had entered the White House, and it began to be suspected that Seward and Chase, as well as Douglas, might have to be content with the fate of Henry Clay and Daniel Webster – that the Republican candidate in 1860 would be a dark horse, not so dark as to be invisible, but not so light as to attract the attention of the public too soon and too obviously. Whatever presidential ambitions Lincoln had cherished since 1856 he had now less reason than ever to suppress ; he might still say that he would prefer six years in the Senate to four in the White House, but there was no chance of entering the Senate – and there was some of entering the White House.

CHAPTER VI

THE CANDIDATE : 1858–1861

Speech at Cooper Union — the Chicago convention — President
elect – The impending crisis.

NEXT year Lincoln took an opportunity to
advertise himself in the East. His eldest son was
at school at Exeter, New Hampshire, preparing
to enter Harvard. Robert Lincoln was not as
zealous a student as his father had been, and
Lincoln went east to stimulate his son to exertion
and managed at the same time to be invited to
address a great public meeting of the Republican
party in New York. It was eleven years since he
had spoken for Taylor in the East ; then an
obscure party hack, he was now a well-known if
not yet a leading member of his party. His
Cooper Union speech was very successful. Despite
his western accent and awkwardness of manner,
there were astute observers in New York who saw
his abilities ; but very few of them can have
imagined that the tall and homely westerner was
to be the victor in the conflict for the Presidential
nomination, a conflict which most people con-
sidered was already settled in favour of the senior
Senator from New York, William H. Seward.

Lincoln would, of course, be put forward by
Illinois as her " favourite son," but many of those
who expected to vote for Lincoln at the beginning
of the Republican Convention thought of it as
a purely formal honour. There were others,
however, notably Herndon and David Davis, who

had more serious hopes.   After all, Lincoln had
real assets.   He was not quite obscure, and yet
he had not played an important enough part to
make enemies.   He could be represented as a
typical poor boy who had made good, a rebuke to
the aristocratic pretensions of the South and an
indication that the Republican party was heart
and soul democratic.   Had not Dennis Hanks
providentially found rails which Lincoln and he
had split thirty years before ?   These rails were
to be the log cabin of the appeal to the great
heart of the American people !   But it was not
enough to be an honest, capable rail-splitter.
The presidential nomination was won less by
appealing to the people than to the professional
politicians, although, of course, ability to make a
popular appeal was an asset the professional politician prized.   Other considerations were potent
in the actual manœuvring before and during a
convention, and Lincoln's friends showed themselves masters in this delicate art.

When the convention met at Chicago on May
16th, 1860, it was obviously Seward against the
field.   Lincoln's managers proposed to try to
concentrate on Lincoln all the fears and resent-
ments that Seward's predominance aroused.
The fact that the convention was held in Lincoln's own state helped a little, for the galleries of
the " Wigwam " were full of his supporters, but
more important were the bargains made with the
leaders of the delegations of other states, bargains
in which seats in the Cabinet were promised in
exchange for votes.   There were three ballots, and
on the third Lincoln secured a majority of the
delegates.   Lincoln was sitting in the telegraph

FL

office at Springfield when the great news came through ; he accepted the enthusiastic acclamations of his friends and left at once to tell Mary Lincoln that, barring some extraordinary accident, she would be what she had always dreamed of being – the wife of the President of the United States.

The nomination was in fact equivalent to election, for the Democratic party was torn in pieces, and the same party feuds which had endangered Douglas in his senatorial campaign now denied him the Presidency. The Democratic convention at Charleston split, and the southern extremists nominated Breckenridge of Kentucky, while the northern Democrats nominated Douglas. This split made Republican victory inevitable, and produced yet another party, headed by John Bell of Kentucky, which ran on a simple programme of " Union and Constitution," appealing chiefly to the old Whigs and, by taking their votes away from Douglas, making Lincoln's election doubly sure.

Despite the gallant asseverations of his official biographers, the choice of Lincoln as Republican candidate was startling to the country and frightening to the more far-seeing members of the party. The split in the Democratic ranks made the chances of Republican victory overwhelming, and, while no one could be certain what action the South would take once the victory of its enemies was certain, there could be no doubt that a crisis at least as serious as that of 1850 was approaching. In such an emergency, all the legal powers of the executive would be in the hands of a country lawyer with no practice in administration, and one whose sole experience of federal government had been an undistinguished term in the House of Representatives. Outside Illinois little or nothing was known of him : it was to be hoped, at best, that he would be a tolerable figurehead, and that he would let greater men run the country. There were men who knew better – Douglas, for instance – but, as election day drew near, the signs of storm grew more obvious, and doubts as to Lincoln's ability to weather the storm became more urgent – and he could not fail to be elected ! He received, it is true, a great deal less than half the votes cast, but as the vote was counted by states, and as he carried all the northern states, he would have been elected even had all the opposition votes been concentrated on Douglas. This possibility, in itself, gave some basis to southern complaints of sectional rule, since it showed that a sectional majority, which was a minority in the whole nation, might capture the executive, and with it power to do harm to the " peculiar institution." On the other hand, the congressional elections had produced a majority opposed to the Republican platform, and there were abundant possibilities of preventing the new administration from doing irreparable damage to southern interests, if the Democrats in Congress played their cards well. These possibilities were so obvious that few outside the South (and not all in the South) took seriously the threats of secession made by the extremists. They had heard such threats before, and they were as willing as the Asquith Government in the case of Ulster to take them as bluff. They were regarded as bargaining-points, as threats designed to force the Republicans to make compromises that would take the sting out of their victory. It was the business of the statesmen who had not committed themselves too deeply on either side to build a bridge of gold on which the noisier politicians, North and South, could meet. That the President-elect would agree to any plausible bargain that could be arranged was taken for granted by the world at large.

But to the inner circle of his friends and party Lincoln was already showing that he knew his own mind. He refused, repeatedly and in unmistakable words, to "compromise of any sort on slavery extension." He would not consent to any such adjustment because, as he told a southern correspondent, "You think slavery is right and ought to be extended ; we think it is wrong and ought to be restricted." On this simple point all negotiations broke down : the official reason for existence of the victorious party was opposition to the extension of slavery ; the economic or psychological need for at any rate formal possibilities of slavery extension was the driving-force behind the southern extremists. On that point they had split their party, rejected Douglas, and made it certain that Lincoln would be elected. But the arts of the diplomat and the lawyer might possibly have triumphed again, the cracks might have been papered over, and it is possible that if the war had not come in 1861, it might never have come at all. Lincoln ended whatever chances there were of that way out. He rejected for himself, and for his party, the various devices for evading the issue that came out of the committees of Congress and out of the Peace Congress which Virginia organised. As far as any one man was responsible for a decision which might involve war, it was Lincoln. He was polite ; he was willing to give all assurances that the federal Government would respect all rights guaranteed under the constitution ; but in his view those rights were a good deal less than the most moderate southern opinion claimed.

It is true that in doing this Lincoln did not believe that the secession of the southern states was serious. He shared the illusions of the greater part of his party on this point, but it is highly probable that, had he foreseen the future, he would have made the same decision. He believed that there were things worth fighting for ; that democratic government could only survive if it clung to its legitimate authority as firmly as any other form of government did. If a federal republic could exist only on the basis of a club – as long as the members did not choose to resign – it was no Government, and it was to be head of a Government that Abraham Lincoln had been duly elected. He would be faced in that office with grave difficulties, but he was determined to face them, with plenty of pliancy in detail but with complete firmness in principle. If the South was bluffing, he would call the bluff; if, as he thought unlikely, the South was in earnest, so was he. In the four months which one of the least fortunate devices of the constitution left to the dying and repudiated Buchanan administration, decisions were taken which made certain that Lincoln, on his inauguration, would have that resolution put to the test. Until March North and South were groping in the constitutional twilight ; what was imminent was fairly plain to see, but few could bear to see it.

CHAPTER VII

SUMTER : 1861

The approach of war – the question of the forts – the first
inaugural – " bread to Anderson " – war.

BOTH sides in the impending war suffered from
illusions which were natural but expensive. The
federal Government, the northern population,
and the President were afflicted by that blindness
which is the first state of Governments and nations
faced with a rebellion. They refused to believe
that the majority of the white population of the
South was in favour of secession. The machi-
nations of Jefferson Davis and other conspirators
had been so far successful that ordinances of
secession had been passed, armies were being
raised, and Union sentiment was hidden, but no
doubt it was there, awaiting the re-establishment
of federal authority to encourage it to manifest
itself ! Over the greater part of the South there
was in fact no important section of the population
(the slaves excluded) which was loyal to the
Union, once secession was an accomplished fact.
The old order withered away, and, by the time
Lincoln was inaugurated, federal authority had
ceased in seven states (although the federal mails,
by a sensible tacit compromise, continued to
function for a few weeks longer). The character
of the federal Government made this revolution
easier than most. There were no local police
forces or other means of coercion in federal hands.

There were, with few and unimportant exceptions, no federal garrisons. There was no Dublin Castle, no Monjuich, to be taken or to survive, an island of legality, in the revolutionary sea. With the formal secession of the state Governments, the outward signs of the authority of the United States simply vanished. But it was thought the bluff of the southern leaders could be called, and, once it was called, there would be an uprising of loyalty in southern hearts which would confound the prophets of doom.

The southern calculations were equally fallacious. There were numerous voices in the North which greeted the departure of the South as a good riddance. To the Abolitionists of Garrison's school, the great evil of slavery had been the compulsory sharing of another's sin which the Union imposed on the free North. The " agreement with hell and covenant with death " was now broken, and the secessionists could be left to stew in their own juice, to repent their sins on the burning marl of the new confederacy. The North had cleared its conscience of the perilous stuff. To the most important northern journalist, seceded states were erring sisters who should be left to go their way in peace. Mr. Greeley, for the moment, was opposed to rescue work on behalf of these Magdalens. To practical politicians, like the eminent lawyer Caleb Cushing, secession was an accomplished fact. Then there were the voters who had not wanted Lincoln as President and who were not distressed to see the triumphant party in a hole, and who awaited a lead from the only man in the country whom they trusted, Stephen Douglas. Last, and most important, were the average men who, in voting for Lincoln or for any other candidate, had not fully understood that they were taking part in the first act of a revolution, and were quite at a loss as to their rôle in the second act which was opening. All this confusion of sentiment and of understanding seemed to justify the optimistic southerners who were sure that the North would not fight and seemed to give grounds of belief to the vigorous orators who suggested that northern passivity was due to cowardice, to those demoralising effects of commerce and industry that had been noted by such thinkers as Mr. Tennyson. The two great southern arts (almost their only arts) had been oratory and law ; oratory warmed their hearts and an excessive devotion to legality muddled their heads. They were sure that they had a good legal case (they had) ; they forgot that the place for good legal cases is in court-rooms, not on real or even potential battle-fields. Long forced, by their isolation in the western world, to hide their own fears and doubts under extravagant assertions of superiority and overwhelming confidence, they were to discover how very expensive the flattering unction of illusion can be to a society that acts on it.

There were few relics of federal authority in the lower South by March, but there were some. The army of the United States was only 17,000 strong ; it was mostly doing police work on the western frontier ; but there had been a small concentration of troops in Texas and a few small garrisons scattered in forts outside various southern harbours. The troops in Texas capitulated under a convention ; most of the small forts and

arsenals fell into southern hands ; but Fort
Pickens, in Florida, and the forts in Charleston
Harbour remained in the hands of the federal
Government, and thus, instead of a slow series of
negotiations and manoeuvres, destined to influence
public opinion on both sides, instead of a situation
in which a *fait accompli* of completely successful
secession would face the new President and make
it easier for him to bow (doubtless with many
face-saving gestures) to the inevitable, both sides
were forced to make decisions whose import could
not be hidden from the world. If the northern
Government allowed the garrisons at Fort Pickens
and Charleston to be starved out, the retreat from
the formal duty of any regular Government could
not be concealed. It would be one thing for Mr.
Lincoln to admit, in practice, that the jurisdiction
of the federal courts in South Carolina was at an
end ; the federal officials had resigned, it was
impossible to serve a writ or impanel a jury, and
it was difficult, if not impossible, to collect customs
duties. But the issue presented by the forts was
simple and dramatic. There the flag of the federal
Government still flew ; there were officers and
men of the federal Government performing their
duties. To abandon them was to throw up the
sponge, to admit at once an inability on the part
of the new President to carry out his oath of office :
"to take care that the laws be faithfully executed."

On the southern side the case was almost
equally clear. To permit a " foreign government " to occupy the harbour of the spiritual
capital of the Confederacy was to run a risk of
appearing ridiculous. On that point South
Carolina would fight.

She had, in fact, already fought. A series of negotiations had gone on between the retiring President and agents of South Carolina with a view to preserving the *status quo*. South Carolina had no desire to act alone, and Buchanan, a good, easy man, had no desire but to avoid trouble during the few months that the constitution left him of office. Whether Buchanan betrayed the confidence placed in him by the " commissioners " from South Carolina does not matter much, for the initiative was taken out of his hands by the action of Major Anderson, commanding in Charleston Harbour, who, on December 26th, moved his little garrison from the quite indefensible position of Fort Moultrie to the more tenable position of Fort Sumter. Buchanan's Cabinet went through another crisis ; the northern members overruled their feeble chief and decided not to order Anderson back to Moultrie, and also to reinforce him in Sumter. A merchant steamer, *The Star of the West*, with 200 soldiers and military stores, was despatched to aid Anderson ; it entered Charleston Harbour on January 9th ; it was fired on by the secessionist batteries, and, unsupported by the garrison of Fort Sumter, to whom its coming and errand were a surprise, it steamed off. The first shots of the Civil War had been fired, but the American people, legally minded, awaited the inauguration of the new President before paying attention to the firing on the national flag. For the remaining two months of Buchanan's term, Fort Sumter was unmolested, and no attempt was made by the federal Government to reinforce it. Fort Pickens, off Pensacola Harbour in Florida, was held in the same way.

The organisation of a southern confederacy went
on. A temporary constitution for the seven
seceding states was adopted on February 8th, and
next day Jefferson Davis was elected President of
the Confederate States of America at Mont-
gomery, Alabama.

When Lincoln took the oath of office on March
4th, 1861, the crisis was too serious to be explained
away on the simple theory of bluff, but there was
still hope of peace, and, perhaps, of union. In his
inaugural address, Lincoln asserted that the Union,
" in contemplation of universal law and of the
constitution," was perpetual, and that he was
bound by his oath to preserve it. The decision of
peace or war lay, therefore, in southern hands,
for, " You can have no conflict without being
yourselves the aggressors. You have no oath
registered in heaven to destroy the Government ;
while I shall have the most solemn one to preserve, protect, and defend it." He ended with an
appeal to the old love of the Union which he
hoped was still potent in the South, for " the
mystic chords of memory, stretching from every
battlefield and patriot grave to every living heart
and hearthstone all over this broad land, will yet
swell the chorus of the Union when again touched,
as surely they will be, by the better angels of our
nature."

In picking his Cabinet, Lincoln had shown a
sense of his responsibility to the country by in-
viting into it men who had seemed, a few months
before, to have far more chance of being President
than he had, and who were still startled by the
odd working of the popular will. Seward,
after some hesitation, had agreed to be Secretary

of State, a post which he thought – and said – would be equivalent to that of Prime Minister. Chase had unbent to become Secretary of the Treasury, and Edward Bates of Missouri, to his contemporaries a great man, was Attorney-General. The Cabinet, then, was strong in personalities ; it united in its bosom almost all the leaders of the party, and this was a source of political strength, if of administrative weakness. If there was to be a war, the heads of the War and Navy Departments would be very important offices indeed, and, for the navy, Lincoln had agreed to accept Gideon Welles of Connecticut, largely on the suggestion of the Vice-President, Hannibal Hamlin. Welles turned out to be an excellent choice, and his reputation for administrative capacity and honesty was in dramatic contrast with that soon acquired by the Secretary of War, Simon Cameron of Pennsylvania. Cameron's presence in the Cabinet represented one of the bargains made without Lincoln's knowledge at Chicago. Cameron was the first of a great dynasty of Republican bosses, a master in the tenebrous politics of his state ; but his methods, or those of his associates, were so excessively practical that the news that Cameron was destined for the Cabinet provoked very impressive protests. Lincoln tried to get out of his offer but Cameron exacted his pound of flesh and accepted the War Department as the best he could hope to get since the idea of making him Secretary of the Treasury had been abandoned.

The worries incident to the planting of Cameron in the Cabinet were only exaggerated examples of the office-seeking plague which raged in

Washington in the early months of the administration. The Republicans, coming into power for the first time, had an especially ravenous horde of deserving party men to be given the spoils of the defeated Democrats. The Government departments, weakened by the desertion or sabotage of southern officials, were now weakened further by the replacement of experienced officers by newcomers, and the President had little time to think of the nation while he was pursued by ruthless job-hunters all over the White House. The new Minister to England, Charles Francis Adams, as a devoted admirer of Seward and as the head of the most distinguished and self-admiring of American families, had a poor enough opinion of the new President, but, when he was taken to see Lincoln before his departure for London, he expected *some* general directions for his mission. If there was going to be war, keeping Britain neutral would be as important a task as commanding the army or navy. All that the President said to him was to disclaim any credit for nominating Adams, that was Seward's doing – and then he turned to the Secretary and announced, with satisfaction, that he had settled the Chicago post-office trouble ! Adams left the White House in despair. But Lincoln saw the incongruity of his position as well as anyone, and compared himself to a man letting rooms at one end of a house while the other end was on fire.

How far the fire would spread and how to put it out were questions in Lincoln's mind every waking moment. His energetic "Prime Minister" had plans, however, and was sure that Lincoln would do as his real superior and nominal subordinate told him. Indeed with the exception of the Postmaster-General, Frank Blair, all Lincoln's Cabinet began their service with a feeling that their chief was not likely to be fit for his job. Lincoln's two predecessors had been very weak Presidents, and it might well have seemed the only hope for the country to reduce the nominal head of the executive to a mere chairman and to put the Government into commission. Seward was convinced that unless he were allowed to run the Government it was doomed. He still hoped that a peaceful settlement with the South was possible, and was anxious to avoid any conflict. Consequently, he engaged in negotiations with the agents of South Carolina who had come to discuss the Sumter question which they took as a tacit recognition of their rank as ambassadors and as an undertaking that the *status quo* in Charleston Harbour would not be altered ; that is to say, that reinforcements or supplies would not be sent to Sumter. But, whatever ambiguities Seward's diplomacy introduced into the already complicated situation, Lincoln had made up his mind to " send bread to Anderson," and, in fulfilment of a promise made, sent notice to Governor Pickens of South Carolina of his intentions. The next move was with the South. Should they await the northern expedition and take their chance of repelling it, with the inducement that Sumter might be surrendered before the relief expedition arrived, or should the batteries prepared for the attack be loosed on the fort ? The advocates of decisive action won ; they feared, or professed to fear, that, unless there was some obvious breach with the

North, the whole secession movement would collapse and South Carolina would be left isolated. Moreover, the refusal of the border slave states, especially Virginia, to secede had been a bitter blow, and an attack on Fort Sumter would create a new situation. The decision was taken and at 4.30 on the morning of April 12th the Civil War began. The bombardment of the fort and its return fire did little damage that day, and the besieged and besiegers had a new distraction ; for a small federal squadron had arrived off the bar. This was the expedition of which Lincoln had warned Governor Pickens, but the chief vessel destined for the relief expedition, the *Powhatan*, had gone off to Fort Pickens, thanks to Seward, who had added naval operations to his duties, off his own bat. The ships did nothing, the bombardment was renewed the next day, the barracks in the fort caught fire, and Anderson surrendered. The only death was that of a Confederate soldier, and that was a result of firing a salute ! But the bloodless contest was of vital importance. Lincoln had forced the South to strike the first blow, and, as Toombs, the Confederate Secretary of State foresaw, that blow stirred up the hornets' nest.

On April 15th Lincoln called on the state governors to provide 75,000 volunteers. His proclamation refused to recognise the fact that there was a great rebellion to be faced ; it talked only of combinations resisting the law and the troops were called out to enable " the laws to be duly executed." The response was decisive – both ways. The border states protested at this attempt to force them to " coerce " their sisters. Virginia, North Carolina, Tennessee, proceeded to pass ordinances of secession, and the decision of Maryland, Kentucky, and Missouri seemed only postponed. The aggressive party in the South seemed to have justification for their action. But the hornets now poured out of the nest. There was no more talk in the North of letting the erring sisters go in peace. The President had asked for 75,000 men; he could have had double or treble the number ; and, along with the proclamation, went out the news that Douglas had visited the White House and declared his support of the President. When Lincoln read his inaugural he had not known where to put his hat, and with a gesture Douglas had held it for him. Now he redeemed the promise of the gesture, and his personal following in the North was far more numerous and far more loyal than that of any other man. There is a story that a leading " Douglas Democrat," passionately opposed to the " Black Republicans," went to tell his leader that he was off to join the Confederate army – and left him to join the Union army. The story is but a dramatic version of what happened to tens of thousands of men all over the North ; the cause in a moment ceased to be that of a party and became that of the nation. Lincoln's patience with the South and his final resolution " to send bread to Anderson " were now justified. He had won the first trick.

For the moment, the situation of the Government was both humiliating and dangerous. The capital lay between two slave states, one of which, Virginia, had seceded and the other, Maryland, seemed destined to do so soon. The railway to Washington passed through Baltimore, which was enthusiastic for the South, and, as the militia began to arrive, it was assailed in the streets. There was no protection against a *coup de main* for some days, save for a handful of regular troops and hastily collected recruits. Lincoln's composure nearly broke down, but the South was unprepared to take its chance of beginning the war by adding Washington to Fort Sumter. The militia, for all its zeal, was a far from reliable support. It had been neglected in the North, and the efficiency of its regiments ranged from fair to farcical. Acting under an Act of 1795, the troops were only called out for three months, and they were organised and officered by the state governments as seemed best to the governors, few of whom had any serious idea of their responsibilities. But Congress was called for July 4th, and on May 3rd Lincoln called for 40,000 three-year volunteers, doubled the regular army, and added 18,000 seamen to the navy, actions of doubtful legality which Congress hastened to ratify. The federal Government had shown commendable energy, and, under the advice of the veteran commander of the army, Winfield Scott, it showed great wisdom, for it offered the command of the new army to Scott's fellow-Virginian and favourite pupil, Colonel Robert E. Lee. Lee disbelieved both in slavery and secession, but he felt bound to go with his state. His decision was a triumph for the South, a disaster for the North, and added to the short list of examples of a commander-in-chief having had the choice of sides. If he had lost Lee and Virginia, Lincoln was resolved to hold the other border states. Federal authority had to be asserted in Maryland to secure the

GL

capital, but there was no violent coercion of the state ; Kentucky was allowed to preserve a perilous neutrality, and the Unionist party in Missouri was supported as far as was possible. None of these states seceded, and, in the long run, Lincoln's policy justified itself. The western part of Virginia, which had little but a legal connection with the rest, refused to allow formal secession to cut it off from the Union, and Lincoln was able to help it to separate its fate from that of the rest of Virginia. The brief and almost bloodless campaign in which this was done made a hero out of George B. McClellan and damaged the reputation of Robert E. Lee. It also enabled Lincoln to preserve the fiction that there was a " loyal " state of Virginia represented by the government of Francis Peirpoint. Frémont was sent to St. Louis to rally the Unionists there, in which he was not very successful, but, all in all, the Government had done well. The general public, however, thought it had done singularly little.

CHAPTER VIII

BULL RUN AND McCLELLAN : 1861–1862

THE army of short-term volunteers in Washington was eating its head off. Horace Greeley, the chartered oracle of northern sentiment, issued a stirring leading article to the refrain of " On to Richmond." The secessionist bluff should be called at once and the rebel capital taken ; its existence, only a hundred miles from Washington, was an insult ! Despite the misgivings of the aged General Scott, commander of the army and veteran both of the war of 1812 and of the Mexican war, an advance on Richmond was ordered. The job was entrusted to General McDowell and the volunteers who had saved Washington. The campaign was to be a picnic, and many of the northern troops wore fancy costumes like those of a modern fraternal order. The two armies met at Bull Run or Manassas.[1] Both were too raw to carry out the manœuvres planned for them, and the battle was a scrambling series of combats to decide which side would break first. It was a near-run thing, but the North lost. Spectators who had driven out to see the fun were swept back to Washington by the panic-stricken fugitives. Bull Run was more than a defeat ; it was a national humiliation. It convinced all the

[1] Many battles of the Civil War have different names in the North and South.

best people in England that the Union was doomed ; the Yankees had turned out the braggarts they had been suspected to be, and " public opinion," in the press and in the clubs, declared for the South.

Very expensive southern illusions were fostered by the victory. The belief that any southerner could whip two, three, or even ten " Dam' Yankees " was confirmed. This belief helped to prevent any exploitation of the victory. Like Hannibal after Cannæ, the South waited for surrender. The chance of seizing Washington, and thus winning the border states, and perhaps, European recognition, was lost. Of course there were difficulties in the way. Bull Run had been won by an army with two commanders, Beauregard and Joe Johnston, and the speedy arrival of President Davis on the scene further complicated the question. But, even if all these commanders had agreed on a pursuit and exploitation of the victory, the condition of the southern army was almost as bad as that of the routed Federals. On the whole the completeness of the southern victory turned out badly for them. It lulled them into security and it stimulated the North into purposeful action, into the creation of a real army. That task was entrusted to the young man whose success in a series of skirmishes in western Virginia had shone like a good deed in a naughty world.

The relations of Lincoln and the new commander of the " Army of the Potomac," George Brinton McClellan, make the most disputed episode of his Presidency. Some of the facts are beyond dispute. McClellan was an admirable organiser. The days of " three-month volunteers "

in fancy clothes were over. The troops were now
enlisted for three years and put on a less casual
footing in supplies and organisation, as well as in
uniform. The work McClellan did in making
an army out of a mob won the praise even of his
enemies, and he made numerous enemies every
day of his command. Camps were organised,
officers were called back from the metropolitan
delights of Washington to their regiments, and
the making of regiments out of mobs and of divi-
sions out of regiments went on, with what, looking
back, seems astonishing speed. McClellan had
the unanalysable gift of inspiring confidence in
his men. Before they had ever fired a shot under
his command, the soldiers adored " Little Mac "
and believed him to be indeed a " young Napoleon." Lincoln and his Cabinet, startled by Bull
Run, were as struck by McClellan as were the
soldiers. He was a hero, the saviour of his country. It would have been too much even for a
less vain man. McClellan was only thirty-four ;
after a very promising career in the army, he had
resigned as a captain to become a railway man-
ager. He now found himself on top of the world,
not after a painful climb but through having been
dropped there from a balloon.

Though so recently returned from civil life, he
had that maddening contempt for civilians which
soldiers so often display. The contempt was not
confined to McClellan ; it was shared by so great
a captain as Sherman, but Sherman did not flaunt
it and Sherman kept out of politics with vehement
ostentation. McClellan did not. He was a
Democrat ; so were his intimates ; they were
willing to make any sacrifice to save the Union,

but had less than no care for what might befall
the Republican party or its programme in the
process. To a great many politicians, the republic and the Republican party were the same
thing. An end of the war which meant a compromise with the South, a restoration of the
Union as it had been, was ominous for politicians,
whose future depended either on the destruction
of the politically opposed South, or the continua-
tion of the sectional controversy. Such politicians
became suspicious on very little provocation, and
McClellan gave plenty.

The task of training an army seemed to the
North to take an absurdly long time. " All quiet
on the Potomac " from a reassuring bulletin became an increasingly bitter joke. The approach
to Washington by sea was blocked by the rebel
army. " *Les Allemands sont à Noyon* " was the
standing reproach to governmental complacency
which Clemenceau kept at the head of his paper
for the first three years of the last great war. The
same reproach was felt by the North, and by the
President, at the sight of rebels across the Potomac. General Scott, like Lord Kitchener, predicted a long war. He was in favour of elabo-
rate encircling movements, nicknamed the
" anaconda." Such plans were an insult to
American optimism, but McClellan would have
been better advised if he had imitated Scott's
pessimistic candour. Either because he was not
altogether free from illusion himself, or from a
hesitation to trust politicians whom he already
disliked and despised, McClellan fell into the
bad habit of promising speedy and vigorous
action without any real attempt to implement his

promises. He also made the great mistake of despising Lincoln. He was abominably rude to him, and, what was worse, he was querulous and secretive in his dealings with him.

While McClellan was training his army, the navy was being rapidly expanded and was beginning to make the blockade more than a fiction. In the general despondency at the absence of news on land, the North was electrified to learn that on November 7th, 1861, Captain Wilkes had held up the British mail steamer *Trent* and had taken off her Messrs. Mason and Slidell, who had been sent to London and Paris to secure recognition of the Confederate states. The capture of the eminent rebels was received with hysterical joy, but it involved the Government in grave difficulties. The omission to take the *Trent* into port and have it condemned by a prize court gave Palmerston a chance to score off the American Government, even if it meant reversing his own position. Northern opinion was already bitterly resentful of the ostentatious sympathy for the South displayed by the better classes in England. In the early days of the administration, Seward had suggested picking a quarrel with one or more European Governments in the hope that North and South would unite in this common war. Lincoln had killed the idea, which was dangerous enough, and he had brought Seward round to his point of view : that foreign intervention must be avoided at all costs. The South must not be allowed to gain her independence by the method that had won the independence of the United States.[1] It

[1] It should be remembered that Seward's project was, in essentials, that attributed to the Ministers of George III by

was a delicate diplomatic situation, but Lincoln and Seward got out of it with as much grace as they could. They surrendered the envoys, noting that Britain had adopted American views of the freedom of the seas ! But the climb-down was too obvious to be concealed by any dialectical ingenuity, and the North clamoured for action.

Lincoln had put up with McClellan's caution and accepted, however reluctantly, the reasons for inaction in which the general was so fertile ; but at last he took the initiative and ordered a general advance for Washington's birthday (February 22nd). McClellan, who was, since November 1st, commander of all the northern troops, naturally disliked moving to a programme fixed by political as much as military considerations. He forgot, as soldiers so often do, that war is only part of politics. Lincoln himself was not wholly a free agent. His party was getting more nervous and more radical. Congress had appointed " a joint committee on the conduct of the war," and the executive had to deal with this rival body as well as to handle the susceptibilities of the general-in-chief. Lastly, the Secretary of War, Simon Cameron, had gone. A master of machine politics, he was less competent as a military organiser. His Pennsylvania political associates were accustomed to a broad and flexible outlook on public accounting, and to some of them the war seemed a good thing and their connection with Cameron a means of getting in on the ground floor. Cameron may have deserved a more glowing tribute to his honesty than that given him

Vergennes in 1777 and used by him as a means of inducing Louis XVI to recognise American independence.

by the Senator who said, "The Secretary would not steal a red-hot stove," but he was incompetent, at the best.

His successor was an old acquaintance of Lincoln's, the arrogant Pennsylvania lawyer, Edwin Stanton, who had since acquired some fame as one of the loyal members of Buchanan's Cabinet. He was ill, irritable, unjust, and not above deceit; but he was not only rigidly honest in money matters himself but had an excellent nose for dishonesty in others and a terrific power of work. He had been, or represented himself as having been, a particular friend and admirer of McClellan's, but, as the war showed no signs of being finished by a bold advance by the Army of the Potomac, he came to regard its commander as an obstacle to victory. It happened, then, that when McClellan moved at last, his vigour was suspect and soon his loyalty was questioned. The plan finally adopted was that of a transference of the army by water to the estuaries below Richmond. The rebel army had retreated from before Washington, and Mc-Clellan's slow advance in its wake had irritated the Government. Lincoln had grave doubts of the wisdom of an indirect attack on the Confederate capital which involved the danger of leaving Washington without the protection of the army. McClellan underestimated the political importance, not only of real safety for the capital, but of apparent safety. For his own peace of mind and security of command, he ought to have done everything possible to reassure his civilian chiefs. This simple duty he neglected. If his peninsular campaign had been crowned by speedy success, that would not have mattered, but McClellan was a slow and careful soldier. It is easier to sympathise with him now than it was before 1914. To-day, after the bloody lessons of Passchendaele, Morhange, Verdun, the reluctance of McClellan to throw his troops against entrenchments, as a " thruster " would have done, seems less contemptible, and his careful exploring of the ground, his preference for manœuvre, his reluctance to believe that the enemy only required a vigorous enough assault to collapse, seem to us to show a prescience as to the effect of modern weapons that is now more creditable than it then seemed to the impatient strategists of the newspaper offices and government departments.

McClellan was too much of a pessimist, but his pessimism was better justified than the optimism of some of his superiors. It had one great drawback : it ignored the feverish expectations of the North, expectations that were bound to have an immediate effect on the administration. As the Army of the Potomac moved very slowly up to Richmond, the brilliant campaign of Stonewall Jackson in the Valley of Virginia frightened Washington. McClellan was deprived of his post as commander-in-chief and some of the troops on which he had counted were made into a separate army. Johnston, commanding the confederate army before Richmond, was wounded, and succeeded by the military adviser to President Davis, Robert E. Lee. Lee boldly called Jackson in from the west and attacked McClellan. On June 26th began " the Seven Days." In this series of battles, the Confederates attacked again and again. Lee's losses were far greater than McClellan's ; his army's trust and devotion were unshaken, but the movement south to a new base on the James River, although appearing masterly at this distance of time, seemed to the North, and to Europe, a disastrous retreat.   When the great advance had begun in the spring, the world had seen the Confederacy as doomed.   Now it saw the attack on the rebel capital repulsed.   At what cost these successes had been achieved few suspected, although Lee himself had few illusions ; his future, like Ludendorff's in the early summer of 1918, was " brilliant but without prospects." But public opinion in the North, in Congress, and in the Cabinet, could not stand the strain. The Army of the Potomac was recalled to Washington.

CHAPTER IX

Pope and Second Bull Run – Antietam and emancipation – the
    end of General McClellan – the congressional elections –
    Fredericksburg.

LINCOLN was now in a position of extraordinary
difficulty. He had tried McClellan and that
young man had, as he had been persuaded, failed
him, but it was hard to find a substitute. Still,
if things were dark in the East, there was more
cheering news from the West. There had been a
number of successes there which brought some
fame to a general called Pope and, to the surprise
of most of those who knew him, to Ulysses
Simpson Grant. Grant had been educated, like
most of the generals of the Civil War, at West
Point, where he had not shone, but he had done
well in Mexico. The career of a peace-time
officer did not appeal to him, and Captain Grant
had to resign his commission as a result of too
much drinking. Unmilitary in manner, in
appearance, he was remarkably " unsoldierly " –
except on the battle-field. Rising rapidly in the
western armies, to which nobody in the East
paid much attention, he scored the first great
federal success of 1862 by capturing Forts Henry
and Donelson and 15,000 prisoners, thus thrust-
ing the Confederate frontier away from Kentucky.
His reputation was so bad in official circles that
when the news came that he had won, with difficulty, a very bloody battle at Shiloh, his superiors

were ready to believe he owed his escape to luck and gave all the credit to Grant's formal superior, Halleck. That officer was known as "Old Brains"; he was a learned soldier of the Austrian type, whose career proved that the pen is mightier than the sword, for by writing despatches he cashed in on Grant's victories in the shape of the post of chief military adviser to the President. He spent the rest of the war in his office in Washington, writing minutes and scratching his elbows when asked any definite question.

At the other end of the great Mississippi river system, Captain Farragut, a sailor of Catalan origin, had taken New Orleans at the head of his squadron. The greatest city of the South was captive and both ends of the Mississippi waterway thus in federal hands. But these successes in the eyes of the world, and of the nation, counted little as long as northern authority ceased on the Potomac. It was becoming more and more important not to give the governments of Europe – that is, the two great maritime Powers of Britain and France – any excuse for armed mediation. A decisive victory in the East was what the South needed. That would do for them what the capture of Burgoyne at Saratoga had done for the revolted colonists. Such a defeat meant the ruin of the Union.

It was in these circumstances that John Pope, a flashy general from the West, was given an army formed out of what Jackson had left of the minor federal armies in Virginia and of troops drawn from McClellan's army slowly coming back to Washington. Pope insulted his army in a proclamation which hinted that they were now at last to be shown real fighting and which announced that his headquarters would be in the saddle. Lee, delighted to have to do with this *miles furiosus*, is said to have remarked that he thought the saddle a better place for the hind quarters, and, at the second Battle of Bull Run (Second Manassas), hopelessly defeated Pope (August 29th–30th). The game seemed to be up, and there was, in fact, only one way out, a way so humiliating that most of the politicians dismissed it as inconceivable. But Lincoln had at last learned that he must be President; that the responsibility was his and that he might as well have the power too. He recalled McClellan to defend Washington, then gave him command of all the troops he could collect, to stop Lee, who was invading Maryland.

Gideon Welles, the Secretary of the Navy, noted with disgust that the troops passing to the front cheered as they passed McClellan's house, but ignored the White House and the President. Many politicians were already convinced that McClellan had allowed Pope to be crushed, that he did not want a victory. The congressional elections were only two months off; if a decision could be postponed till then, the administration might be ruined and McClellan dictator. But Lincoln refused to believe that McClellan was a traitor, and he took the responsibility. The general's own position was not enviable, for he had only the President's word to authorise his taking command ; his troops had been handled in a fashion to excuse a serious loss of fighting spirit and he was facing an army and a general with whose achievements all the world was ringing.

The invasion, if it succeeded, would end the

war. The northern morale could not stand another defeat and, even if it could, the fatal intervention or mediation of France and England could not be long delayed. A strong party in the British Cabinet agreed with Napoleon III that the time had come to end the futile conflict which was causing so much trouble to commerce simply because the North would not recognise the inevitable. It needed just one more victory to decide Palmerston and Russell. Moreover, the invasion of Maryland was expected, in the South, to bring that state over to the Confederacy. There were plenty of southern sympathisers in Maryland, but the most ardent of them were already fighting in the Confederate army. The state was not really bound up with the slavery system as closely as southern theorists believed ; and although, in one of the worst of all patriotic songs, Maryland had been summoned to join her seceded sisters, "for thy dalliance does thee wrong," the sight of the ragged southern soldiers was no more welcome to many theoretical secessionists than the sight of the Highlanders in the Forty-five to many a loud-swearing and hard-drinking English Jacobite. If the imminent battle was a southern victory, then the " baffled tyrant spurns amain " would be a sentiment heartily homologated by Marylanders, who would rush to the aid of the victors. The fate of Maryland, of Washington, of the Union, depended on Mc-Clellan. His arrival had had a magical effect on the troops, and, for a moment, there was a chance that Lee and Jackson, separated from each other, would be crushed in detail ; for the southern orders, wrapped round a cigar, had been found in the street. McClellan moved cautiously, but not necessarily too cautiously. Like Jellicoe at Jutland, he might lose the war in a day.

The battle, when it came, found Lee's army concentrated, but McClellan remained master of the field. Both sides lost heavily at Antietam, but it was the most important of northern victories all the same. It was high tide for the South, her last chance of imposing peace on the North. Henceforward the war was a test of mere endurance, with most of the assets for such a contest in northern hands. McClellan *had* saved the country; unfortunately, he knew it and said so. His success gave his enemies fresh breathing-space, and politics were now, reasonably enough, in the forefront of all minds. The congressional elections were a month off, and the administration would have to give an account of its stewardship. It was not a cheering prospect. The high hopes of the spring had been withered. The South had recovered from its panic; had invaded northern territory both in east and west, in Kentucky as well as in Maryland, and had nearly ended the war at a blow. If it had not, the credit was due to a general in notorious political disagreement with the administration.

In the first months of the war there was little or no dissent from the Government's war programme. Politicians who continued to palliate southern treason or to talk of local imitations of it, like Sickle and Fernando Wood in New York City, had to repent quickly. The example of Stephen Douglas was powerful. But Douglas had died in July and the suppression of the rebellion seemed more than a promenade, and the cause of the North not merely an exertion of legitimate authority, but a crusade of fanatics who had got control of the Union by a minority vote and were now exploiting their authority to violate the constitution. Tens of thousands of northern soldiers hated a " nigger-lover " at least as much as they did a rebel. They had not enlisted to free the slaves, and regarded any suggestion that they had as a betrayal of their loyalty and a justification of the southern claims. This point of view was strong in the Army of the Potomac and in McClellan's *entourage*.

On the other hand, the longer the war lasted, the more obvious it was that slavery was at the bottom of southern separatism and that slavery was turning out a military asset. For one southern fear had been proved groundless – the nightmare of a slave rebellion. The slaves worked patiently and loyally while their masters fought, thus freeing thousands of whites for the army. On the other hand, the approach of northern armies was too much for old loyalties, and the problem of dealing with the fugitives was urgent. It was soon seen to be ridiculous to send back slaves to help their masters to rebel more efficiently. Generals acted as they thought best, some with an absurd regard for the legal rights of the owners, others with an eye to popular applause from the militant wing of the Republicans. One ingenious soldier found the solution of treating the slaves who escaped to his lines as contraband of war, and, from the spring of 1862 on, slavery began to crumble away wherever northern armies were established on southern soil. But there was the problem of the

HL

border slave states who had stayed in the Union, but whose position had become very difficult. Lincoln tried to induce them to adopt compensated emancipation, with federal aid, but with mulish obstinacy their representatives refused this statesmanlike offer. Slavery was abolished in the District of Columbia ; Seward, abandoning a position that American diplomacy had defended for a generation, made a treaty with Britain allowing mutual search of suspected slavers and thus made possible a real, as apart from a nominal, end of the slave-trade ; but the cry for general emancipation, for the uprooting of the upas-tree, grew stronger as the Union hopes grew fainter.

Greeley, having recovered from the momentary depression which the result of accepting his advice to press on to Richmond had produced, now demanded from Lincoln an affirmative answer to the " Prayer of Twenty Millions " – that is, the abolition of slavery. Lincoln told Greeley that slavery was a secondary question. " If I could save the Union without freeing any slave, I would do it ; and if I could save it by freeing all the slaves, I would do it ; and if I could save it by freeing some and leaving others alone, I would do it. What I do about slavery, and the coloured race, I do because it helps to save the Union ; and what I forbear, because I do not believe it would help to save the Union." From this point of view he did not budge, although party pressure increased. Clerics who came to tell him that they had information that it was God's will that he should free the slaves were asked why God had not communicated His wishes directly ; but, jest or no jest, the political need for emancipation was great.

The paradox of fighting a war without talking about its cause, or promising to root out the source of so much bloodshed, could not go on for ever.

Emancipation would seem a betrayal to millions of Democrats, but these citizens and voters were already being alienated by the length of the war and the inevitable strains and fractures the constitution was undergoing. On July 22nd Lincoln announced to the Cabinet that he had not called them to ask their advice but to lay before them a proclamation emancipating the slaves. All the Cabinet except Blair and Bates, who came from border states, approved, but Seward was opposed to issuing it in the moment of defeat, saying that it would seem " our last shriek on the retreat." Lincoln at once agreed ; and the proclamation was laid on one side. Antietam, if not a brilliant victory, was at least the end of a great military crisis, and the chance was taken. On September 22nd the Cabinet was again summoned, and after Lincoln had read the latest " piece " of Artemus Ward's, he spoke of a promise he had made "to myself," and, hesitating a little, " to my Maker," that as soon as the rebels should be driven out of Maryland, he would issue the proclamation. The text was amended a little, but not in any important detail. By virtue of his power as *ex officio* commander-in-chief, Lincoln declared that all slaves in territory in rebellion against the United States which had not submitted to proper authority by New Year, 1863, were freed. The proclamation was the public acknowledgment that the Civil War was no longer a contest over constitutional interpretation, but a revolution. Its importance, for the moment, was symbolical, for, as critics at home and abroad were quick to point out, slavery was only abolished in those parts of the country where the federal Government had no authority. But the proclamation was no empty word. It was a pledge of future action, and it doomed slavery to extinction in the border states ; not at once, but inevitably, if the Union survived the war.

The political effects of the proclamation could not be helpful as long as the military situation continued bad. Only victory could give strength against peace Democrats and Republican radicals. McClellan had again displayed his caution, his great weakness, " the slows," as Lincoln put it. He would have been more than human if he had not been resentful of his treatment and if he had not distrusted the hostile and not too trustworthy Stanton. He fell back on his procrastinating policy ; instead of insisting on a free hand, he negotiated and promised, and finally only moved under orders ; even then he moved very timidly. On November 7th, 1862, McClellan was at last removed, and this time for good. To the historians of a generation after the war, the removal was fully justified. McClellan had been tried fully and found wanting. It is not so easy to decide to-day ; the pursuit of the enemy after Antietam on the model of Murat after Jena, or Blücher after Waterloo, no longer seems so easy. More decisive still is the consideration that McClellan's hold over the trust of his troops was as great as ever. The soldiers knew that under "Little Mac" they fought battles which might not end in complete victories, but which were great improvements on First and Second Manassas, and that the balance of losses was in the favour of the North. A few more victories or semi-victories like the Seven Days, not to speak of Antietam, would ruin the Confederate army. Lee shared this view. For him McClellan was " by all odds " the ablest northern general he had to face all through the war. But politics demanded that the Army of the Potomac be separated from its maker, for the elections had come and had been an exceedingly narrow squeak. Before Antietam, Maine had held its elections, a famous political barometer. The Republicans had won, but by an ominously narrow margin, and, more ominous still, the Democratic candidate for governor who had done so well was no "War Democrat," but a peace man – a " Copperhead," to use the hostile nickname. It took no special insight to guess what would have been the effect of a defeat instead of a formal victory ! Even with the victory, the elections had revealed an astonishing growth in hostility to the administration and the war.

Lincoln kept control of Congress, but only because the border states had been induced to vote for him by rough and ready means. Only in New England and in the far West was there a real majority for the war. In New York a distinguished soldier was beaten by the Democratic candidate, Horatio Seymour, and the control of the greatest state in the Union passed into hands hostile to the administration, and, it was suspected, not paying more than lip-service to the Union cause. All the middle states followed New York ; the results were a humiliation to the administration and an invitation to foreign powers to intervene, since the North was no longer united.

One last attempt was made that year to win victory. McClellan's successor was Ambrose Burnside, known as a good dancer and as the possessor of magnificent side-whiskers, but not thought by his fellow corps-commanders, or even by himself, fit to command the army. There were none of McClellan's slow movements or timidly careful examinations of the ground in Burnside's campaign. He adopted the administration's own plan of an advance straight on Richmond and on the rebel army, if it got in the way. Lee blocked his passage at Fredericksburg, a formidable position on the south bank of the Rappahannock. Burnside sent forward wave after wave of troops, whose astonishing gallantry, notably that of the Irish brigade, won the admiration of their foes, who had the simple task of shooting them down. Like July 1st, 1916, December 13th, 1862, showed what new troops can be trained to endure. Burnside lost over 12,000 men, Lee 4,000.

It was lucky for Lincoln that he had not removed McClellan a month sooner ; Fredericksburg, although a mere repulse and not the complete disaster a defeat in Maryland would have been, would yet have been quite enough to turn the elections. Burnside, with the obstinacy of bad generals, was willing to try again, but the Army of the Potomac had had enough, and, after some floundering in the mud, Burnside was replaced by Hooker, one of the corps-commanders who had a fair record and the advantage of not having got on with McClellan. The last illusions of the politician were shattered and the unfortunate army was left to lick its wounds in winter quarters. The dreadful year was over, and Lincoln never knew another as terrible. His second surviving son, Willie, had died, and the death had shaken the not too stable mind of Mary Lincoln. The failure of his administration seemed evident. He had few friends or supporters, even in his own party, and the pressure from the radical wing was getting stronger. Seward was now loyal and useful, but was politically a source of weakness, since to the radicals he was the origin of those conservative counsels on which the blame for defeat was being put. Chase, eaten up with ambition, was convinced that the mistake of 1860 would be repaired in 1864, and that the party would return to its senses and make the best man President. Lincoln knew of Chase's ambition, and knew that Chase thought very little of his chief and was in constant touch with the hostile radicals. He gave no sign of resentment, but, when the senatorial cabal called on him to dismiss Seward, he displayed all the political skill which he possessed. Chase, who was a party to the conspiracy, was rash enough to offer his resignation formally, and Lincoln seized the precious paper before Chase could retreat. The President had already secured Seward's resignation, and, when the deputation delivered its ultimatum, Lincoln had, as he said, " a pumpkin at each end of the bag." He forced Chase to disavow his allies, and kept both Chase and Seward in the Cabinet. He was at last master in his own house. His authority was never questioned in his Cabinet again, and the attempt to transfer control of the Government from the President to Congress was baffled. If the Union was to be saved in the next two years, it would have to be by the President, and Lincoln, for all the disasters of the war, had no doubt that he was better fitted for that task than anybody in sight. Against all pressure, he stuck to his determination to issue the definitive proclamation of emancipation, in appearance more a mere manifesto than ever since Fredericksburg, and, on January 1st, the slaves in the revolting states were declared " for ever free."

CHAPTER X

THE DARKEST HOUR : 1863

The Monitor and the Morrimac – Gettysburg – Vicksburg – Chattanooga – " government of the people, by the people, for the people."

THE year 1862 ended in gloom, but the situation was not quite as black as it seemed, although there was further disaster yet to come. At sea, federal supremacy was unquestioned, since the spring when, for a few nerve-racking days, the menace of the *Merrimac* had hung over Washington. The *Merrimac* (or *Virginia*) was a federal war vessel, sunk when Norfolk Navy Yard was abandoned. The Confederates had raised her and converted her into an ironclad. Thus made formidable, she had sallied out to attack the great wooden fleet that lay off Norfolk, and sank what she chose to attack. If unchecked, she would break the blockade and cut McClellan off from his water-borne supplies. But the federal Navy Department had not been caught napping, and its new ironclad, the *Monitor*, had arrived in time to drive the *Merrimac* off. Henceforward, Confederate naval operations were confined to the defence of rivers or harbours and to commerce-destroying. This activity was made possible by the narrow interpretation of the duties of a neutral adopted by the British Government. Southern cruisers were fitted out in British yards under the most transparent disguises, but Lord Russell refused to take action. When the overwhelming evidence of the character of a very formidable one was brought to his notice, the legal question involved was referred to a law-officer whose madness was not yet public property. By the time it was recognised, the *Alabama* had put to sea, and she sank sixty-nine vessels – for which the British taxpayer had, ultimately, to pay. Lincoln, Seward, and the admirable diplomat, Charles Francis Adams, whom they had sent, more by luck than by design, to London, effected their purpose ; they avoided giving the British Government an excuse to intervene, and, at the same time, they recorded their dissent from the ideas of neutrality current in London. With Antietam the danger of an unprovoked intervention passed ; the South needed an " incident," and it was the business of the administration to see that they did not get it. That business at least was admirably done.

The new commander of the Army of the Potomac got it into shape fairly quickly, and if his headquarters were, as Charles Francis Adams the second acidly declared, a combination of a " brothel and a bar-room," they inspired more trust than had the morally blameless headquarters of Burnside. There was some hope, if not much confidence, when, in April, Hooker advanced, but it was short-lived. Lee sent Jackson round Hooker's flank, and the Battle of Chancellorsville was as humiliating a defeat as Second Manassas. Northern despair of a successful end of the war grew and was reflected in the rise of Confederate credit in Europe. The only bright spot was the death of Stonewall Jackson, shot by his own troops in the dusk.

Lee began to prepare for another invasion of the North. A victory in the North, the cutting

of the communications of Washington and
Philadelphia, had a good chance of undoing
Antietam. But the invasion was not a plan that
appealed to Davis ; there were no hopes now of
" rescuing " Maryland, and thousands of men
were kept in scattered garrisons all over the
South instead of being sent forward to give Lee
overwhelming strength. Nevertheless the news
that Lee had crossed the Potomac was full of
menace. Lincoln decided that the Army of the
Potomac could not be trusted to fight under
Hooker, and, indeed, rumours were rife that he
was to be removed. When the troops heard a
rumour that McClellan had been recalled they
burst into enthusiastic cheers, but it was not to
McClellan that Lincoln turned. A messenger in
the night awakened a corps-commander, George
Gordon Meade, and assured him that he was not
being arrested, as he had feared, but was to take
command of the army. On the first three days of
July was fought the Battle of Gettysburg, and the
little town in Pennsylvania saw the invasion
defeated. Without Jackson, Lee was no longer
invincible in attack. It was a battle like Waterloo,
but there was no rout on one side and no pursuit
on the other. Lincoln was delighted at the victory
and bitterly disappointed at the failure to exploit
it, but he did not remove Meade.

Gettysburg was not the only northern triumph.
In London, Adams had pointed out to Lord Russell
that ships were still being built for the Confederacy.
They were not mere cruisers, but rams, ships of the
type that Tegethoff was to use three years later
to such effect at Lissa. They were being built
in a neutral country, and " it would be superfluous

in me to point out to your lordship that this is war." But the threat was unnecessary, Russell had already ordered the detention of the rams. The intervention crisis was over for good. If the South was to win, she would have to win unaided by Britain and, therefore, by France. Another federal victory had been won in the streets of New York, where a mob, mainly Irish, had risen in rebellion against the draft. Conscription had become a necessity, but the method adopted, which allowed the rich to buy exemption, was a peculiarly odious one. Many an eminent American in the next generation owed his start in life to the foresight and capital which had enabled him to hire a substitute to do his military service. Lincoln kept his own eldest son out of the army till the last few months of the war, for fear his death might drive his mother mad, and, when he did send him to the army, he took care to see he was on the staff. There were real grievances behind the riots, though not enough to justify their savagery. But troops from Gettysburg were hurried to the city and the draft enforced. Lastly, on July 4th, Vicksburg surrendered.

Vicksburg was a small town on bluffs above the Mississippi. It had acquired great military importance as the citadel of Confederate strength on the great river, and the slow and apparently vacillating movements of the attacking army had worried Lincoln a good deal. But General Ulysses Grant had managed at last to get into a position to besiege it and now it had surrendered. "The Father of Waters flows unvexed to the Sea," said Lincoln, for the only remaining Confederate river stronghold, Port Hudson, followed the example of Vicksburg. It is a common-place to say that the Confederacy was cut in two, but that mattered little. The states west of the Mississippi were not very important, although Texas had the advantage of having an international frontier with Mexico and so could help to defeat the blockade. But the Mississippi was not like a European river ; it was wide and deep enough to float a fleet – and it did. The capture of Vicksburg was comparable, not to the seizure of a bridge-head like Mayence or Ratisbon, but to the seizure of the Dardanelles or the Channel ports. Henceforward, the North could use its naval power on the western as well as on the eastern flank of the Confederacy.

The year ended with a more dramatic victory still, for Grant, in his most brilliant campaign, redeemed the mistakes of Rosecrans, rescued the army besieged at Chattanooga, and, storming the heights, drove the lately victorious army of Braxton Bragg in rout before him. At last, Lincoln thought, he had found a general. The change in the fortune of war helped the President. His Cabinet was now reconciled to his authority and the public to his eccentricities, although his indecorum of speech was still deplored. He was in the habit of answering serious men in an apparently frivolous fashion, and, though one witness says that he never heard Lincoln tell an improper story,[1] there is a mass of contrary testimony. He played what were really practical jokes on dignified persons. When an over-zealous military commander arrested the leading peace Democrat, Clement Vallandigham, Lincoln disapproved of

[1] Thurlow Weed.

the arrest but felt himself bound to back up the general. He accordingly sent the martyr into the Confederate lines ! This helped to turn what might have been a scandal of military usurpation into a joke, and when the enraged Democrats of Ohio ran Vallandigham as their candidate for Governor in the autumn of 1863, he was badly beaten.

Lincoln had no illusions about the political necessities of the case. It was now the third year of the war, and most of the Democrats who put the Union above all other con-siderations had become Republicans, or closely allied with them. Had Douglas lived, he might have held his party together, but emancipation and the more and more obviously revolution-ary character of the war alienated millions. Despite the suspension of *Habeas Corpus* and the defiance of the courts when they tried to limit military jurisdiction, opinion was freely expressed, there was only a sporadic control of the press, and the terror which raged during the world war would have horrified the most determined Republicans. In the border states and in the southern parts of Illinois and Ohio there were hundreds of thousands of southern sympathisers who skirted, if they did not cross, the verge of treason. In Missouri and Kansas the war de-generated into a savage guerilla campaign, and the great bandits of the 'seventies, the " James Boys," learned their trade while raiding for the South. The hand of the federal Government was sometimes heavy in such regions ; there were arrests that were hard to justify, and the press and the pulpit were hampered. Appeals had to be made direct to the President for relief from zealous officers who proposed to bar from their pulpits ministers who were suspect of disloyalty!

In all such questions Lincoln showed masterly tact. He knew, as a politician, that he had to please or conciliate voters, and, if they were hopelessly alienated, they would undo at the polls any victories won on the battle-field. He was both too humane and too wise to let the full rigours of military law be inflicted, and there was a constant tussle between him and Stanton over the enforcement of discipline in the army. Lincoln showed a lawyer's adroitness in discovering reasons why soldiers should not be shot for disciplinary reasons, and there was more than adroitness in his evasion of what was to the righteous Stanton his obvious duty. He had been noted on the frontier for his hatred of cruelty to animals ; he became noted for his hatred of cruelty to humans. Yet he wanted the war to continue : he thought the suffering worth the reward, victory.

In this autumn of 1863, when things were beginning to go well, he made an opportunity to re-state his view of what the war was about. There was to be a formal dedication of a military cemetery at Gettysburg at which the famous orator, Edward Everett, the best Greek scholar in America, was to speak. Lincoln invited himself and prepared his speech on the train from Washington. Even Everett's ornate eloquence palled after two hours, and, when the President rose to speak, the crowd had scattered and, by the time the stragglers had got near the platform, the speech was over. The audience was puzzled and disappointed, and no one, certainly not the eloquent Everett, realised that the most famous of American orations had just been delivered and that future generations would find it fit to be compared with the speech of Pericles over the Athenian dead.   Lincoln had spoken for two minutes these words: "Four score and seven years ago our fathers brought forth upon this continent a new nation, conceived in liberty and dedicated to the proposition that all men are created equal.

" Now we are engaged in a great Civil War, testing whether that nation or any nation, so conceived and so dedicated, can long endure. We are met on a great battle-field of that war. We are met to dedicate a portion of it as the final resting-place of those who have given their lives that that nation might live.   It is altogether fitting and proper that we should do this.   But, in a larger sense, we cannot dedicate, we cannot consecrate, we cannot hallow, this ground.   The brave men, living and dead, who struggled here have consecrated it, far above our power to add or to detract.   The world will very little note nor long remember what we say here ; but it can never forget what they *did* here.

" It is for us, the living, rather, to be dedicated, here, to the unfinished work that they have thus far so nobly carried on.   It is, rather, for us to be here dedicated to the great task remaining before us ; that from these honoured dead we take increased devotion to that cause for which they here gave the last full measure of devotion ; that we here highly resolve that these dead shall not have died in vain ; that the nation shall, under God, have a new birth of freedom and that government of the people, by the people, for the people, shall not perish from the earth."

CHAPTER XI

Lieutenant General Grant — the Wilderness — " the war is a
failure " — Farragut — Sherman — Sheridan — victory in sight.

THE task of establishing government of the people
by the sword was now entrusted to Ulysses Grant.
For him was revived the rank of Lieutenant-
General, hitherto held only by Washington. To
him was given command of all the armies, subject
only to the President. He was freed from Stanton's control, and Lincoln resolved to give the
new general full confidence. After some hesitation, Grant rejected the advice of his chief lieutenant, Sherman, and left the western front for
the East. Sherman took over in the West and,
although Meade was left in nominal command of
the Army of the Potomac, it was evident that
Grant had come to measure himself with Lee.
The boldness of that undertaking he gravely
underestimated, and, although he displayed a
tact which had been lacking in the egregious
Pope, his arrival was not too warmly welcomed
by the eastern troops. Victory in the West was
easier and cheaper than it was in the East. So
thought the Army of the Potomac, and they were
soon proved right.

In April Grant advanced south, attempting to
manœuvre past Lee. That general was necessarily on the defensive ; he was greatly out-
numbered, and he rose brilliantly to the occasion.
The battles fought in the brushwood of the
Virginian " wilderness " were desperate and

IL

bloody. Grant, with the complacency of the fighting general, announced, when hopes of an easy victory had vanished, that he " would fight it out on this line if it took all summer." But although he had superior numbers, although his losses could be replaced while Lee's could not, the army tired of these desperate assaults on the Confederate trenches, of these flank marches which always found Lee in position. The bloody spring became the bloody summer, and, when the morale of the army had been badly damaged and after the troops had first attacked with the gallantry of despair and then had refused to attack at all, Grant had got to Petersburg, where McClellan had got before. But McClellan had got there by water and by marching and had inflicted heavier losses than he had sustained. Grant had fought his way there, and had suffered losses equal to the whole army under Lee's command. The war of attrition on which Grant had embarked, or found himself embarked, was not an obvious success.

In the West things were not much better. Sherman was too ingenious and unorthodox to hurl his troops on impregnable positions, but his new opponent, Joseph Johnston, was not the general to leave any chances open, so that the advance to Atlanta became a crawl, interrupted by barren manœuvring which left the two armies as they were. If the North and Lincoln could have had world enough, and time, the pounding tactics of Grant, the musical chairs of Sherman, would have been no crime, but 1864 was an election year, and, if there were no improvement in the military situation by November

it was not hard to guess how the accounts submitted would be taken.   Discontent was rife in
the Republican party, and the radical wing toyed
with the idea of running Frémont as a sort of
" ginger candidate."   That scheme came to little,
since it was obvious that if the Republicans could
not win with Lincoln, they could win with nobody.
The Republicans took the name of the " Union "
party, but the Democrats were not placated, and
their appeal to the country was summed up by
Vallandigham : " The war is a failure."   It
seemed a platitude that the war *was* a failure, and
Lincoln wrote a brief memorandum :

" *August 23rd, 1864.*
" This morning, as for some days past, it
seems exceedingly probable that this administration will not be re-elected.   Then it will be my
duty to so co-operate with the President-elect,
as to save the Union between the election and
the inauguration ; as he will have secured his
on such grounds that he cannot possibly save
it afterwards.

" A. LINCOLN."

This document he had signed by the Cabinet, but
without permitting them to read it.

A week later, the Democrats, as Lincoln had foreseen, nominated McClellan.   The candidate denounced the defeatist platform, but the policy of the
South was obvious.   If the war could be spun out
until after November, and if neither Richmond
nor Atlanta had then fallen, the administration
would be beaten.   It was a war of attrition indeed, not in the crude butcher's arithmetic of

Grant, but in the more subtle attrition of the will to victory. There was a price the North was not willing to pay for victory, and that price was almost reached in the summer of 1864. It is not, indeed, as certain as Lincoln assumed that the election of McClellan *would* have meant the end of the Union. The South was very weary too, and since it had left the Union because of a Republican victory it might have been ready to return after a Republican defeat. Slavery was mortally wounded, as more and more of the southern leaders realised, and McClellan, who was too good a soldier not to see the great military assets possessed by the North, might have negotiated a peace under the threat of a continued war. But, be that as it may, the only southern chance was to postpone all military decisions until November. Jefferson Davis refused to do this. He removed Johnston, whom he disliked, and replaced him by a " fighting general," Hood. Hood attacked, and, in a few weeks, Atlanta was in Sherman's hands – a great triumph militarily, economically, and politically, for it opened the western flank of the Confederacy. As he had done two years before, Lee used the " covered way " of the Shenandoah Valley to threaten Washington, and, with grosser culpability than McClellan's, Grant almost delivered Washington to Jubal Early. If Early had had a little more nerve – and luck – Lincoln might have had to flee. Grant learned his lesson and sent Philip Sheridan to stop up the bolt-hole. In a brilliant and ruthless campaign, Sheridan destroyed the Confederate army and wasted the valley so thoroughly that " a crow crossing it would have to carry his rations." Sherman, cutting loose from Hood and his own communications, began his march " from Atlanta to the sea " right across the Confederacy, destroying and burning, teaching the rebels that " war is hell." Farragut took Mobile, the last confederate port on the Gulf of Mexico, and, off Cherbourg, the *Alabama* was sunk by the *Kearsarge*. " Sherman and Sheridan have knocked the bottom out of the Chicago platform," said the exultant Republicans.

In November Lincoln was re-elected, but, even in the flood-tide of victory, McClellan polled a vote dangerously large for the peace of Republican minds. Had the news from the front been defeat instead of victory, the Republicans would have been ruined, and were the seceded states to enter the Union on the old terms, the Democrats north and south would rule the nation again. The thought was intolerable. The radicals in Congress had already forced Lincoln to let the conservative Blair leave the Cabinet. They had violently assailed Lincoln's attempts to get the conquered parts of the South into the Union on easy terms, and, in the crisis of the summer of 1864, the Wade-Davis manifesto had attacked the President with extraordinary bitterness. As the end of the war drew palpably nearer, Lincoln felt more and more anxious that it should end leaving as few scars as possible. He had always been tolerant of peace " feelers," as long as the Union was the basis accepted by both sides ; this necessary preliminary had hitherto been a stumbling-block, but was there not some hope that the southern leaders would see that their cause was lost ? Sherman had reached the coast and had taken

Savannah and Charleston. Thomas, whom he had left behind, had annihilated Hood's army at Nashville, and, though Lee still held the trenches of Petersburg, the inferiority in numbers, the shortage of food, and the steady advance of Sherman from the south, made his position untenable for long.

In a last effort to avoid unconditional victory, Lincoln went to Hampton Roads, where, on February 3rd, he met the Confederate delegates on shipboard. Chief of them was the Vice-President of the Confederate States, Alexander Stephens, whom Lincoln had known and admired when both were ardent Whigs in Congress. But the southern delegates had nothing to offer ; they still clung to the hope of independence – and that, less now than ever, could Lincoln concede. The obstinacy of Davis was the greatest crime this upright and determined man committed against the people he served so devotedly. Slavery was dead ; in a few weeks the Confederate Congress would arm slaves and free them. Independence was a hopeless cause, but there was yet time to save something from the wreck by surrendering on terms. The chance was lost, and Lincoln had to go back to Washington to face the complete victory obviously brought nearer every day. March 4th came again, and, for the second time, Lincoln took the oath of office. He was an older man by more than four years. The permanent melancholy of his temperament was now marked by his lined and weary face, and it was not with exultation that the pilot who had weathered the storm addressed his people :

" Fellow Countrymen : At this second appearing to take the oath of the Presidential office, there is less occasion for an extended address than there was at the first.   Then a statement, somewhat in detail, of a course to be pursued, seemed fitting and proper.   Now, at the expiration of four years, during which public declarations have been constantly called forth on every point and phase of the great contest which still absorbs the attention and engrosses the energies of the nation, little that is new could be presented.   The progress of our arms, upon which all else chiefly depends, is as well known to the public as to myself ; and it is, I trust, reasonably satisfactory and encouraging to all.   With high hope for the future, no prediction in regard to it is ventured.

" On the occasion corresponding to this four years ago, all thoughts were anxiously directed to an impending civil war.   All dreaded it – all sought to avert it.   While this inaugural address was being delivered from this place, devoted altogether to saving the Union without war, insurgent agents were in the city seeking to destroy it without war – seeking to dissolve the Union, and divide effects by negotiation.   Both parties deprecated war ; but one of them would make war rather than let the nation survive ; and the other would accept war rather than let it perish.   And the war came.

" One-eighth of the whole population were coloured slaves, not distributed generally over the Union, but localised in the southern part of it. These slaves constituted a peculiar and powerful interest.   All knew that this interest was, somehow, the cause of the war.   To strengthen, perpetuate, and extend this interest was the object for which the insurgents would rend the Union, even by war ; while the Government claimed no right to do more than to restrict the territorial enlargement of it. Neither party expected for the war the magnitude or the duration which it has already attained. Neither anticipated that the cause of the conflict might cease with, or even before, the conflict itself. Each looked for an easier triumph, and a result less fundamental and astounding. Both read the same Bible, and pray to the same God ; and each invokes His aid against the other. It may seem strange that any men should dare to ask a just God's assistance in wringing their bread from the sweat of other men's faces ; but let us judge not, that we be not judged. The prayers of both could not be answered – that of neither has been answered fully. The Almighty has His own purposes. ' Woe unto the world because of offences ! for it must needs be that offences come ; but woe to that man by whom the offence cometh.' If we shall suppose that American slavery is one of those offences which, in the providence of God, must needs come, but which, having continued through His appointed time, He now wills to remove, and that He gives to both North and South this terrible war, as the woe due to those by whom the offence came, shall we discern therein any departure from those divine attributes which the believers in a living God always ascribe to Him ? Fondly do we hope – fervently do we pray – that this mighty scourge of war may speedily pass away. Yet, if God wills that it continue until all the wealth piled by the bondman's two hundred and fifty years of unrequited toil shall be sunk, and until every drop of blood drawn with the lash shall be paid by another drawn with the sword, as was said three thousand years ago, so still it must be said, ' The judgments of the Lord are true and righteous altogether.'

"With malice toward none ; with charity for all ; with firmness in the right, as God gives us to see the right, let us strive on to finish the work we are in ; to bind up the nation's wounds ; to care for him who shall have borne the battle, and for his widow and his orphan – to do all which may achieve and cherish a just and lasting peace among ourselves, and with all nations."

CHAPTER XII

PEACE : 1865

The fall of Richmond – surrender of Lee – " bind up the nation's wounds " – John Wilkes Booth – " after life's fitful fever he sleeps well."

THE end of the war was much nearer than Lincoln had hinted in the second inaugural. On April 2nd, President Davis sat in his pew in Richmond, devout as usual, but his devotions were interrupted by a messenger. The President rose and left the church ; the message was from Lee : he was abandoning Richmond. There were still desperate hopes of escaping into the mountains and carrying on the war there, but Grant was vigilant and there was a hot pursuit. On Monday Lincoln came to Richmond and entered the Confederate White House, sitting for a long time at Davis's desk, in profound thought. He came back to Washington more resolved than ever to " bind up the nation's wounds," and when he landed in Washington he told the marine band to play " Dixie," the rebel tune, which he had loved before the war. " The tune is federal property now, and, besides, it is good to show the rebels that with us they will be free to hear it again."

On April 9th, Lee surrendered the Army of Northern Virginia ; his way to the west had been barred by Sheridan, and Grant accepted the surrender with a magnanimity in full accord with Lincoln's policy. That policy was to get the seceded states back to their old status as soon as possible. The freedom of the slaves would have to be safeguarded, of course, for the thirteenth amendment was on its way to adoption, making the emancipation proclamation of unquestioned legal effect ; but otherwise nothing would be done to exacerbate feeling in the defeated section. He had attempted to get Louisiana into the Union on his easy terms, but Congress had refused to let the rebels off so easily. But Congress would be out of the way until November, and, in that six months, the President could do a great deal; his prestige was now great and he hoped to do on his own what even a radical Congress would hesitate to undo.

He called the Cabinet to meet on Good Friday. It was April 13th, four years exactly since Sumter surrendered, and that day General Robert Anderson was to raise the flag again on the fort. It was noticed that the President had seemed to recover some of his old spirits, that since the fall of Richmond he looked less worn. He had been talking during the week of what he would do when his second term was up ; he had saved a little money and would settle down in Springfield. He had read a good deal of Shakespeare in the last few days ; Shakespeare as well as Artemus Ward had been a great consolation in dark days. *Macbeth* was his favourite play, and he had read from it to Sumner, the bitter foe of the South :

> *Duncan is in his grave,*
> *After life's fitful fever he sleeps well ;*
> *Treason has done its worst ; nor steel nor poison,*
> *Malice domestic, foreign levy, nothing*
> *Can touch him further.*

But that was on Sunday last, and on Friday he was in good spirits. " He thought it providential," he told the Cabinet, " that this great rebellion was crushed just as Congress had adjourned. . . . There were men in Congress who, if their motives were good, were nevertheless impracticable, and who possessed feelings of hate and vindictiveness in which he did not sympathise and could not participate. He hoped there would be no persecution, no bloody work, after the war was over. None need expect he would take any part in hanging or killing those men, even the worst of them."

There was only one formidable rebel army left in the field, the troops which Johnston had collected to oppose Sherman. News was expected, and the President was sure it would be good news, "for I had, last night, my usual dream that has preceded nearly every important event of the war. I seemed to be in a singular and indescribable vessel, but always the same, and to be moving with great rapidity toward a dark and indefinite shore. . . . I have had this singular dream preceding the firing on Sumter, the battles of Bull Run, Antietam, Gettysburg, Stone River, Vicksburg, Wilmington, and so on." Grant was present, and objected that Stone River was no victory, but the President went on : " I have no doubt that a battle has taken place or is about to be fought and Johnston will be beaten, for I had this strange dream again last night. It must relate to Sherman ; my thoughts are in that direction, and I know of no other very important event which is likely just now to occur."

That night he went with Mrs. Lincoln to

Ford's Theatre to see *Our American Cousin*. During the third act, John Wilkes Booth, brother of the great actor and an actor himself, entered the box which the guard had left unattended and shot the President through the head, sprang on to the stage, shouting " Sic semper tyrannis," and escaped on horseback – to be caught and shot down by his pursuers a few days later. The President was carried across the street, for he could not be moved to the White House ; he never recovered consciousness, and, at 7.20 a.m., he died. It was Stanton who stood at the bed and, with an unusual ascent into nobility, pronounced the epitaph : " Now he belongs to the ages."

Booth had not been a solitary fanatic ; a conspiracy to murder the leading members of the administration had been planned ; Grant was destined to be a victim, but had left Washington, and Seward, who was in bed as a result of a carriage accident, was attacked and desperately wounded. The plot was one of the most foolish in the history of political assassination. The South had come to realise, very imperfectly to be sure, that in Lincoln they had a very necessary friend at court ; his death not only produced a wave of hate for the rebels, destroying the atmosphere of simple joy that the war was over ; it left the problem of reconstructing the Union in very unfit hands. The Vice-President, who now succeeded Lincoln, was Andrew Johnson of Tennessee, the only southern Senator who had not seceded with his state, and he had replaced Hannibal Hamlin on the " Union " ticket in 1864 as a concession to the " War Democrats."

He was a man of ability, of honesty, of courage ;
but he was reputed to be a drunkard (and reputation was enough), he was violent in language, and
tactless. Worst of all, he had no position in the
party he had so recently joined, and, when he
came to put into effect Lincoln's policy of recon-
ciliation, he was an easy victim for the astute
politicians who led the radical faction.

For the task of making a real peace, all Lincoln's
political skill would have been needed, as well as all
his prestige. In four years in Washington, Lincoln
had added to the stock of wisdom he had acquired
in his obscure days in Illinois. He was a master
politician, combining magnanimity with scepticism. He had in his management of his Cabinet
shown how well he realised that " every man hath
business and desire such as it is," and had
managed to use Seward despite his lapses into
folly, Stanton despite his vile temper and malig-
nancy, Chase despite his pathological ambition.
He had shown the same skill in dealing with
Congress, using the patronage, using flattery,
using the weapons the constitution gave him, to
keep control of the war in his own hands.

The measure of Lincoln's success is shown by the
failure of Jefferson Davis in the same task. It was
not the victories of Grant and Sherman that ruined
the South, but the collapse of the southern will to
resist, and that collapse came because Davis, the
soldier, never knew how to lead a people ; he could
order and beg, but that was not enough. Lincoln
never forgot the one thing necessary, the preserva-
tion of unity of spirit in the North, and for that
he was willing to make all sacrifices of dignity and
of consistency. Early in the war Lincoln's

enemies had sneered that he " would like to have God on his side, but he must have Kentucky." He had kept Kentucky, and more than Kentucky, and so the Union had been preserved.

But that was only the beginning of his task, and the one man who could have made real peace was dead. Lincoln's radical enemies wept for him, perhaps in all sincerity, but hastened to undo what he had begun to do. It was their purpose to pour salt into the nation's wounds, some of them like Sumner from not ignoble illusions, others like Thaddeus Stevens in a hate not unworthy of respect, others with a simple appetite for plunder to which Lincoln and his policy were obstacles. There is no need, so soon after 1919, to describe the men who filled Congress ; there were the hard-faced men who had done well out of the war and were determined and destined to do even better out of the peace. Gideon Welles went on the morning of Lincoln's death to the White House and saw outside it " several hundred coloured people, mostly women and children, weeping and wailing their loss," and this sight affected the unsentimental Secretary of the Navy more than anything else. But indeed something was here for tears, something to mourn. For more than the coloured people, for all America, " untimelier death than his was never any."

BIBLIOGRAPHY

Barton, W. E. :   *The Life of Abraham Lincoln.*
                   President Lincoln.

*Beveridge, A. J. : *Abraham Lincoln, 1809–1858.*

Charnwood, Lord : *Abraham Lincoln.*

Nicolay and Hay : *Abraham Lincoln ; A History.*

Stephenson, N. W. : *Lincoln ; An Account of his Personal*
                    Life.
                    An Autobiography of Abraham
                    Lincoln.

Lincoln's Works, edited by Nicolay and Hay.

The Lincoln-Douglas Debates, with introduction by
G. H. Putnam.

Lincoln's Speeches and Writings (Everyman's Library).

*Adams, J. T. : *America's Tragedy.*

*Morison, S. E. : *Oxford History of the United States.*

*Especially recommended.